DOT ie

DOT ie

A Practical Guide
to Using the Internet in Ireland

Alex French

MERCIER PRESS

MERCIER PRESS
Douglas Village, Cork, Ireland
www.mercierpress.ie

Trade enquiries to Columba Mercier Distribution,
55a Spruce Avenue, Stillorgan Industrial Park, Blackrock, Dublin

ISBN 1 85635 488 1

10 9 8 7 6 5 4 3 2 1

*Mercier Press receives financial assistance from
the Arts Council/An Chomhairle Ealaíon*

Printed and Bound by Colourbooks Ltd

CONTENTS

To my parents, for encouraging me to
waste my youth playing with computers

Acknowledgements

Writing a book is a lot of work, especially for all the people who have to listen to the complaints about how much work it is. A few people deserve a special mention:

I'd like to thank my sister, Tana, who told me to stop talking about this book and write it already. She's in the process of getting her own book finished and we've shared a lot of angst-ridden author moments over the past few months. Without her, I doubt I would have actually started this.

I owe a big thanks to the great people in Mercier Press, who have worked with me for almost a year now with the patience of several saints. I can't imagine it's easy trying to get a first-time author to produce a workable manuscript, but they've been fantastic.

The inspiration for this book came from helping people get online and use the Net over the past eleven years. In particular, my parents provided a never-ending litany of problems for me to solve and the motivation to write down the solutions once and for all.

I should also thank all my colleagues in Bitbuzz, who did my work for me while I finished this manuscript. Thanks guys!

Finally, thanks to Susan for keeping me sane throughout this process. I couldn't have done it without you.

Using this book

Lots of people I talk to have basic questions about the internet and they have a hard time getting them answered: Does it cost anything to send an email? What exactly is a computer virus? What do I need to start using the internet? How do I protect my children online? This book aims to answer these questions and a lot more like them, and take you step-by-step through the online experience.

Everyone has a different level of experience with computers and the internet, as well as different goals for going online. You might want to download music and chat with people on the other side of the world; book airplane tickets; or just email a relative in America. In this book I'll explain how to do all of these things and more.

I don't assume that you know how to use the internet and so chapters one and two cover a lot of the basics. If you have some experience of going online, you can skip straight to the more advanced chapters.

I do assume that you have some basic knowledge of how to use your computer, such as how to turn it on, use the mouse and keyboard and double-click on a program icon, but that's about it. If you want to brush up on these computer skills, I recommend picking up a copy of *The Complete Idiot's Guide to Windows XP* by Paul McFedries. Despite the title, it's a great book covering everything from the absolute basics to more advanced aspects of using your computer. If you use a Mac, try *Mac OS X Tiger for Dummies* by Bob Levitus.

One thing this book *won't* try to do is to make you an internet expert. Although chapter three does cover some advanced topics, my focus is on making you comfortable online rather than getting into technical details or lots of jargon.

In the following chapters you'll learn to use the web, search for information and use email.

Once you've mastered these, you can go on to the more advanced topics in chapter three, where you will learn about things like creating your own web site, using online auctions and buying digital music.

You'll also learn how to avoid some online irritants like unwanted 'spam' email, and how to protect yourself and your family from viruses, online fraud and other internet nasties.

You don't have to read it all in one go; you can dip in and out of these sections as and when you get interested in those topics.

The book is broken up into five sections:
- **Getting Online**
- **The Basics of Web Browsing and Email**
- **Advanced Topics: next steps on the Net**
- **Protecting Yourself Online**
- **Web Directory: great sites to get you started**

Each section is designed to be read on its own, so you can skip or skim through any parts that you already know or that you don't want to get into yet. So if you're already connected to the internet, you can just skip the first section (although you might want to skim through it later to see what your options are). In places where I assume you've read another part of the book, it's clearly referenced.

There's also a glossary of common internet terms at the back, which should help explain the acronyms and technical words that people often use when talking about the Net.

The pictures in the book are 'screenshots' taken using 'typical' software that most people will have on their computer. These pictures might not match exactly what you have on your screen. Every computer has different hardware and different versions of software installed, so your computer may not have every feature I describe (especially if it's newer or older than the one I used) but it should be pretty easy to figure out the differences.

About the sites featured in this book

I've found the web sites featured in this book over the eleven years I've spent using the internet for both work and play. Some of them are great sites, and others are chosen because they illustrate a particular point. Although I think they're all pretty cool, I can't take responsibility for your use of these sites or the services they provide.

None of the web sites featured are connected to this book or have endorsed this book in any way. All web sites and software pictured are copyright and property of their original owners.

All the sites in this book are selected because I like them; it is my policy never to accept money, goods or services in exchange for a web site recommendation, although I am partial to chocolate-chip cookies.

Usage

There is an ongoing debate in digerati circles about the 'proper' way to write many internet-related terms: 'internet' or 'Internet', 'Web' or 'web', 'web site' or 'Web site', 'e-mail' or 'email'. In this book, I've adopted a modern usage which reflects the widespread adoption of digital terms into everyday language. In particular, I spell internet with a small 'i', something that many people still regard as just plain wrong. My usage reflects the fact that the internet is a co-operative, evolving entity without any central controlling body. A capital 'I' would imply one neatly-defined object, capable of being owned and controlled, which the internet most definitely is not. This argument is more eloquently put by Professor Joseph Turow of the Annenberg School for Communication at the University of Pennsylvania, who has launched a crusade to de-capitalise 'internet'. He discusses this issue in an interview with the *International Herald Tribune*.

Similarly, I prefer 'email' to 'e-mail', reflecting the evolution of email from being just an online form of the paper letter into a form of communication in its own right. If you don't like it, send me an e-mail.

Chapter One

GETTING ONLINE

Ready to get online? You'll need a couple of basic things to get up and running:

1. A computer (preferably one that's not too old).
2. A modem: the hardware that connects your computer to the internet.
3. A connection to an internet service provider (ISP).
4. The software that you use to do things like view web pages or send email. This is probably already on your computer.

In this chapter we'll go through each of these and explain what you need and where to get it.

1. YOUR COMPUTER

Your computer is an important part of your internet experience. After all, everything you do online is done through your computer, so you need to make sure it's the right tool for the job.

Just about any computer bought in the last three years will let you get online. But for maximum performance, you need a computer that's capable of running the most up-to-date software so you can access the best of the Net.

Whether you're buying a new computer or connecting an existing one to the internet, it helps to understand what the main parts of a computer do and how they affect your online experience *(if you know how a computer works, you can skip this section)*. Each of the main parts of a computer is listed below, along with an explanation of how computer manufacturers usually refer to them in ads and suggestions for what to look for to maximise your internet experience.

11

PARTS OF A COMPUTER

Memory

A computer has two types of memory:

1. The **hard disk** stores files permanently, even when the computer is switched off.

2. The **RAM** (which stands for Random Access Memory) stores files and programs that are currently in use. In other words, when you're writing a letter on your computer, it's stored in RAM until you save it. When you do save the letter, it will be stored on the hard disk.

Hard Disk

The size of a hard disk is usually given in gigabytes (GB or just G). A modern computer should have a minimum of 40G, but hard disk sizes are getting bigger all the time. You'll need at least 20G to store the basic software you need to use the computer, edit documents and access the internet. The rest is used for the files you store on the computer. The main use for a large hard disk is to store digital music, images or videos, which eat up a lot of space (for example, each gigabyte [G] of hard disk can store around 200 songs). If you're not planning to do a lot of this, don't worry too much about the size of your hard disk.

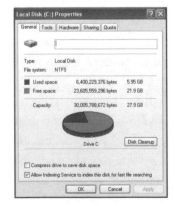

☞ To find out the size of your computer in Windows, go to My Computer, then right-click on the C drive and select Properties. You'll see the total size and the amount of free space you have.

RAM

RAM is the temporary memory that your computer uses to store all the programs and files that you're actually using. RAM is much more important to the performance of the computer than your hard disk. If you use a lot of programs at the same time (for emailing, music, accessing the web), you'll need lots of memory to keep the computer running at a good speed. New programs tend to need more and more memory to run quickly.

RAM is measured in megabytes (M or MB). Newer computers have a gigabyte (1G) or more of RAM (1G = 1024M).

As a rule of thumb, get at least 512M of RAM in a new computer, but 1G (1024M) is even better. You can usually have more RAM added to a computer later if you need to, but this can be trickier with a laptop.

☞ To find out how much **RAM** you have in your computer, click on the Start menu in Windows, and select Control Panels. Then double-click on the System icon (if you don't see this icon, try clicking Switch to Classic View on the left-hand side). The amount of RAM will be shown at the bottom of the window. If it's shown in GB, multiply by 1024 to work out how many MB you have. This screen will also tell you what version of Windows you have (new computers will have Windows XP or Windows Vista).

On a Mac, go to the Apple menu and select 'About This Mac'. Your RAM is shown in the 'Memory' line (very old Macs may not have this option).

Processor

The processor is the part of the computer that does all the hard work, so it has a big impact on how the computer responds to what you ask it to do. The processor generally has two parts to its name: the type and speed. Both are important in determining how a computer will respond.

For a PC, the type of processor will usually be 'Pentium 4' or something similar, sometimes written 'P4'. Avoid the older 'Celeron' processors, which are often underpowered.

For a Mac, recent processor types are 'G4' or 'G5'; the older G3 should be avoided if possible. Apple are now introducing a new line of processors which will be similar to the ones used in a PC. This will make it easier for you to compare the power of a Mac and a PC.

The speed is usually written after the type of the processor. Processor speeds are measured in 'megahertz' (MHz) or 'gigahertz' (GHz). For example, if a computer shop advertises a 'P4 4.3GHz', this means a Pentium 4 type processor running at 4.3 gigahertz.

Since processors get faster every few months, there's no easy way to recommend a minimum speed. If you're buying a new computer but don't want to spend a fortune, the best rule of thumb is to always buy a mid-range processor; this usually gets you good value but helps ensure your computer isn't using old technology.

Screen

A computer's screen is the main way you interact with it, so take some time to consider what you want. There are two things to consider: the type of the screen and its size. The two main types are:

- CRT monitors, which look and work like TVs. They're usually quite bulky but are relatively cheap.
- LCD screens, which are thinner but more expensive than CRT monitors.

Screen sizes are measured in inches, diagonally across the screen. The smallest screens are usually 15' or 17', with the largest reaching 32' or larger. There's usually a big price difference between each size and the next one.

The choice of screen is mainly aesthetic; if you want a big monitor for a good price, a CRT monitor will do fine. If you want something to fit on a crowded desk or look funky in your sitting-room, go for an LCD screen. These days most new computers come with LCD screens anyway.

One other consideration is that LCD screens (especially at the cheaper end of the scale) are sometimes not as quick to respond to changing images as CRT monitors. This can be a factor if you're going to be playing a lot of 'shoot-em-up' games.

Also, remember that the very biggest screens require a special **graphics card** in the computer – that's the bit that the computer uses to display images on the screen. The computer manufacturer or shop should be able to advise you of any special requirements, but you can expect to spend an extra few hundred euro on the graphics card if you're buying a top-of-the-range screen.

Sound

If you're going to be using the computer to watch movies, listen to music or even buy CDs online (see page 100 on buying music online) it's worth getting a computer that can do justice to your music. You can usually get a range of speaker systems with a new computer and prices range from under €50 for a basic pair of speakers to hundreds of euro for full Dolby Surround Sound (great for watching DVDs or playing modern games).

You can add speakers later if you don't get them with your computer but remember that they need a compatible **sound card**, which is the part that the computer uses to send sounds to the speakers. Like a graphics card (see above), you can expect to pay extra for this if you want a really fancy speaker system.

PC OR MAC?

Generally speaking, there are two types of computers that you use at home or in the office. The more common type is usually called a PC, for 'personal computer'. The other is the Apple Macintosh, or just 'Mac'. All computers have some built-in software called the 'operating system' of the computer: this takes care of all the basic tasks that happen on a computer, such as letting you organise files and run programs. The main difference between a PC and a Mac is this operating system: a PC uses the Microsoft Windows operating system, and a Mac uses its own operating system, called MacOS. PCs, which use Windows, are far more common that Macs. You can tell which type of computer you have by watching the screens that come up when you turn the computer on; it will either welcome you to Windows or MacOS.

If you're buying a new computer, you have to choose between a PC and a Mac. When you're making the choice, keep in mind that Macs are easier to use than PCs and are far less prone to viruses and security problems. However, they're also more expensive, and because they're less common, it's not as easy to find software or accessories for a Mac.

Most retailers stock only one type of computer (PCs or Macs) so you'll have to shop around if you want to compare them.

TIPS FOR BUYING A NEW COMPUTER

- Make sure to check the **warranty**. Some manufacturers include it in the purchase price, but with others you have to pay extra. Three-year manufacturers' warranties are usually good value.
- Check what **software** comes with it. You'll need a good word processing program (like Microsoft Word) to do basic tasks like writing letters.
- Get **antivirus** software (see Viruses, page 108). It's often cheaper with a new computer, and may even be included in the price.
- These days, all computers should come with at least two **USB ports** and an ethernet port. These are used for connecting printers, cameras and broadband connections.

- If you will be connecting to the internet using a dial-up connection (see page 20) make sure your computer comes with an internal **modem**. They're cheap as part of a new computer.
- For the best deal, don't buy the most or least expensive **model** in a shop or on a web site; the cheapest is usually old stock that's almost obsolete, and the most expensive is cutting-edge technology that you'll pay a premium for.
- Don't worry too much about other optional accessories – you can always buy them afterwards.

☞ There's also a third operating system you might come across, called **Linux.** This free *open source* operating system is used in company *servers* all over the world. Although it's extremely powerful, it's not as easy to use as Windows or MacOS. It's not often used in home computers, but is slowly gaining popularity as it becomes more user-friendly.

WHERE TO BUY

Computer retailers come and go, so ask around and keep an eye on local press for the best deals.

Dell   www.dell.ie   1850 333 200

Dell is a great place to buy a home PC, since they're good value and often include either a free or low-cost three-year warranty. For the best deals, use the web site to figure out what you want, then ring them to see if they have any special offers – they usually have promotions running on specific models.

Apple   www.apple.com/iestore

If you want to buy a Mac, you can buy direct from Apple. Shipping is usually cheap or free. Pricing tends to be around the same or slightly better than retail Apple shops.

Komplett   ***www.komplett.ie***

Komplett usually has good deals on home computer systems, as well as separate parts and accessories. The company is Norwegian but this web site is specifically tailored for Irish users.

The Laptop Shop ***www.thelaptopshop.ie***   ***01 4759560***

If you're looking for a laptop, these guys can give you advice on models and features direct from their shop in the Stephen's Green Shopping Centre.

O2 Experience Shops   ***01 6705577***
(multiple locations around Ireland)

O2 Experience stores stock Apple laptops and iPods as well as accessories. You can actually try things out in the shop, which is an advantage over online shopping.

2. THE MODEM

To get online, your computer needs a way to physically connect to the internet. This is usually done with a small device called a **modem** which connects your computer to the phone line, cable connection, or something else.

The type of modem that you need will depend on what type of internet connection you want to use. Some modems are built into your computer, others come separately. In the following sections I'll talk about the different types of internet connections, and what kind of modem (or other hardware) you need for each one.

Your internet service provider can help you determine what additional hardware you need, if any. You will often be given this hardware when you sign up for your internet service. For the moment, just keep in mind that you may need a modem in addition to your computer.

3. INTERNET CONNECTIONS and ISPs

Now that you have a computer, the next step is to get it connected to the internet. To do this, you use an **Internet Service Provider**, or **ISP**. Your ISP connects you to the internet and (hopefully) provides you with technical support. Many ISPs also provide you with an email address, although you can always get one later (see Email, page 49).

☞ **How the internet works**

The internet is made up of lots of connected networks run by ISPs, companies and universities. Your ISP's network is one small part of the internet. ISPs and other networks connect to each other using high-speed connections such as fibre optic links. You connect to your ISP and access other computers on the internet through them.

TYPES OF INTERNET CONNECTIONS

There are lots of different ways to connect to the internet. You need to pick the way to connect that suits you in terms of speed and budget. In the following sections I'll go through each of the ways that are commonly used to connect to the internet, as well as a couple that aren't usually used at home but which you might hear people talking about. Then from page 30 I'll talk about how to choose which one's right for you.

Dial-up: This uses your phone line to connect to the internet by making a phone call. Slow but reliable.

ISDN: A faster, digital version of dial-up using a modified phone line.

DSL: Commonly known simply as 'broadband', a DSL connection is a fast, always-on connection to the internet.

Fixed wireless broadband: These connections use a small antenna to connect to your ISP without a phone line.

Cable broadband: You can now get cheap, fast broadband connections over your existing cable TV connection in some parts of Ireland.

Leased line: a permanent high-speed connection used by larger businesses.

Wi-Fi: Provides a wireless connection for laptops in 'hotspots' (hotels, bars, cafes, etc.). Also used within houses or offices in conjunction with DSL.

Satellite: Not as nippy as DSL or cable, but satellite broadband is available where other technologies aren't.

Dial-up

A dial-up connection uses your phone line to connect to the internet. It works by making a phone call to your ISP. Dial-up connections are still the most common way to connect because they're easy to hook up, don't require much special hardware and are cheap if you don't use the internet much. All you need is an ordinary phone line and a **modem**.

Almost all modern computers have a modem built in. (If your computer has one, it will have a small port on the back that looks exactly like a phone socket.) If you don't have a modem, you can purchase one for around €40 in any good computer store.

When you use a dial-up connection, you pay for the phone call exactly as a normal local call. That means connecting to the internet in the evening and at weekends is quite cheap (around one cent per minute).

Disadvantages

The disadvantages of a dial-up connection are:

- You pay by the minute, so you don't know what your phone bill is going to be at the end of the month.
- While you're online, your phone line is engaged and you can't make calls.
- Dial-up connections are quite slow compared to broadband; it can take a long time to download large files, pictures, or music.

Up to a few years ago, most dial-up ISPs charged a monthly subscription fee to use their service. These days, most no longer require you to sign up or pay a subscription; instead, you simply pay for the dial-up phone call (the ISP makes money on your call, which pays for the service).

Some ISPs do offer subscription plans. In exchange for a monthly fee, you can call a cheaper number to connect to the internet. These numbers start with 1891. In addition, technical support is usually provided using a local rate number (1890) rather than a premium rate number (1550 or similar).

It's usually not worth signing up for these plans since the savings are small and you lose the flexibility of switching ISP whenever you want. Before signing up for a subscription I recommend trying out some of the 'free' services. However, if you're going to be calling technical support a lot, you could consider a subscription plan which will give you cheaper access to technical support.

> ☞ Beware premium-rate technical support numbers: it can cost several euro to get a simple technical question answered.

Flat-rate packages

To help you counteract the fear of getting a huge bill at the end of the month, some phone companies have started offering flat rate' packages for dial-up users. These plans enable you to buy a bundle of minutes that you can use to go online at a discounted rate. Most of the packages only give you discounts in the evenings and weekends, but some include daytime internet calls as well. Flat-rate packages can be good value if you use the internet quite a bit on weekends or in the evening.

> ☞ Once you've used the internet for a while and know your surfing habits, consider getting a flat rate package. Check whether the package includes daytime calls (if you need them).

One thing to watch for
Some companies will automatically switch your phone service away from eircom when you sign up for flat-rate internet packages. This means that your phone calls are billed to you by your new provider rather than eircom. Your phone number is not affected. Although most people won't care about this (you may save money on your non-internet calls by doing it), be sure to check exactly what they're going to do before you sign up for a flat-rate plan so you don't get any surprises.

ISDN

ISDN involves upgrading your phone line to two digital lines which can carry information much faster. ISDN never became very popular in Ireland due to the higher costs and extra equipment needed. Since DSL (see below) has become widely available, ISDN has fallen out of favour but it can still be a good option if you can't get broadband. Your line needs to be upgraded to ISDN, and your monthly line rental will double. It requires an **ISDN terminal adaptor** (similar to a modem) which costs €60–€100. Your ISP can recommend or supply a terminal adaptor if you decide to use ISDN. Once it's set up, an ISDN connection works just like a dial-up connection.

DSL

'DSL' stands for **Digital Subscriber Line**, which means it uses your existing phone line, but sends high-speed digital data over it. Although DSL uses your existing phone line, it doesn't interfere with it. You can still make phone calls or send faxes as usual while on the internet.

Many people use the terms 'broadband' and 'DSL' interchangeably, but 'broadband' really means any high-speed, always-on connection, including DSL, wireless broadband and Wi-Fi.

Because DSL is widely available and costs a fixed amount each month, it can be a great option if you use the internet for a few hours each day. DSL is also much faster than dial-up or ISDN.

> ☞ DSL shares your phone line but doesn't interfere with it. DSL uses different frequencies to keep your internet connection separate from your phone calls.

Unfortunately, DSL is not yet available in some areas, and many older phone lines can't support it. To check whether you can get DSL on your line, ring any of the ISPs listed on page 34 and ask them to 'prequal' your line. This performs an initial check to see if DSL is available in your area and also checks the suitability of your line. If your line passes prequal, it's not a guarantee that you can get DSL but it's a good indication. Some ISPs also let you do a preliminary line check on their web site, although this data isn't always 100 per cent accurate.

It usually takes one to two weeks to get DSL activated on your phone line. When you order DSL, you can choose between installing it yourself and getting your ISP to send someone around to do it (an 'engineer install'). Having an engineer install your DSL costs €100 or more, so you might want to try and install it yourself. This is a simple process (you don't need any special tools) and your ISP will usually talk you through it over the phone if you

Checking phone lines for DSL compatability on www.netsource.ie

have questions. Alternatively, a neighbourhood computer-savvy kid may hook up your DSL – see page 37 on ideas for getting help.

If you choose to install your own DSL, your ISP will send you a special DSL modem that connects to your phone line and to your computer. You will also need to connect small **microfilters** to each phone in your house to keep the DSL from interfering with the phone line. These look like small matchboxes and easily connect to the telephone cables. Your ISP should provide simple instructions.

Most DSL connections are 'always-on', so your computer is always connected to the internet. You can just turn on the computer and start browsing the web without going through any connection process.

Some lower-cost DSL connections are 'metered', however, which limits you to a certain number of minutes online each month. If you stay online more than this you pay a per-minute fee to stay connected. With these broadband plans, you need to be sure you know how many minutes are included in your basic fee, and most importantly how to make sure you're disconnected when you're finished surfing – otherwise you'll get an unpleasant surprise when your monthly bill comes in!

Fixed Wireless

If you can't get DSL on your phone line, you can check out some suppliers of fixed wireless broadband. These use a small antenna (smaller than a satellite dish) to connect your home to the ISP's 'base station' (usually located on a high building or a hill).

Wireless broadband technologies are still evolving, and new standards known as **WiMax** will help bring the price of wireless broadband down.

The best wireless broadband connections use fixed antennas permanently mounted on the roof or the wall of your house. These are small and unobtrusive, but you probably require your landlord's permission if you rent your house. The ISP will take care of mounting the antenna and running a cable into your house. Because of the installation work required, wireless broadband connections generally involve an installation fee of a few hundred euro, or a twelve-month contract, or both.

Be wary of smaller mobile antennas that are not permanently mounted on your house. The connection available through these can be of variable quality and you may find the connection slowing down or dropping at times, especially in bad weather. You may need to try putting the antennas in different positions in your house for best results (windows often work best). If you do try one of these systems, make sure that your ISP has service in your area and that you can return the equipment if it doesn't perform well in your house.

A broadband speed comparison from www.clearwire.ie

Cable broadband

Providers of cable TV are now starting to offer broadband packages to their subscribers through the cable system. Because the cable company's equipment in each neighbourhood needs to be upgraded to offer cable broadband, availability can vary quite a lot depending on where you live. You'll need to check with your cable provider to see if it's available in your house. If you can get cable broadband, it's a great option (it's what I use at home). Cable broadband usually offers a better service at a cheaper price than DSL or fixed wireless.

Cable broadband uses a special modem that connects to your computer, like DSL. However, cable broadband usually requires a technician to call to your house and fit the modem. This only takes a short time to do but involves the usual wait at your house between eight and six o'clock.

Leased lines

Leased lines are high-speed connections used in offices. They're permanently connected to the internet and run at speeds ranging from ISDN speeds to many times faster than DSL. Leased lines are expensive and require special equipment, and so are not used in homes or small offices.

Wi-Fi

Wi-Fi is a technology that provides a broadband connection without wires in an area known as a **hotspot**. A hotspot is usually within a building, like a coffee shop, a bar, a hotel or an office block. You can also set up a hotspot in your house so you can use the internet around the house without any wires. Wi-Fi is usually used with laptops, and most new laptops now have a Wi-Fi card built in (if not, a card costs from €30 in any good computer store). All new Apple laptops come with Wi-Fi, and any Windows laptop with the Centrino logo on it has Wi-Fi capabilities.

Public hotspots

Several companies provide Wi-Fi in public places. You can bring your laptop in and access the internet without needing to plug into anything. This is great for meetings or for a quick email check while you're in town.

Using a Wi-Fi hotspot (from www.bitbuzz.com)

Using Wi-Fi in a public hotspot is easy. First, make sure your wireless card is connected (or 'associated') to the hotspot network. To do this, right-click on the wireless icon in your system tray (the group of icons in the bottom-right corner of your screen in Windows) and click 'View available wireless networks'. In the window that pops up, select the network you want to connect to and click 'Connect'.

Viewing Wi-Fi networks in Windows

Now launch your web browser (if you're not sure how to do this, skip ahead to chapter two). If the hotspot you're in requires you to log on, you'll be taken to the login page automatically. Otherwise, you can just browse the web as normal.

Many public hotspots in hotels or coffee shops charge a fee for using the service. You can usually pay online or get a voucher from the staff. Full instructions and details of rates should be available on the hotspot's login page.

Connecting to a Wi-Fi network in Windows

Home Wi-Fi
Wi-Fi can be great for your home as an add-on to a broadband connection. This means that if you have a Wi-Fi enabled laptop, you can use the internet around your home or office without needing to plug into the broadband modem – very handy for surfing the web in the garden!

To set up a hotspot in your house, you have two options: the easiest option is to get a broadband modem with Wi-Fi built in. Most broadband ISPs will provide you with a wireless modem, either for a small additional fee or free of charge when you sign up.

Alternatively, you can connect a wireless **access point** to your existing broadband modem. You can buy a cheap Wi-Fi access point in any computer store or online (and cheaper) at www.expansys.ie. The main manufacturers of access points for home use are Linksys, Netgear and D-Link and a basic model will cost €50–€100.

Installing a home Wi-Fi network yourself can be a tricky process, so try and find a tech-savvy friend to help you. If you do set up a home Wi-Fi network, make sure that it uses proper security. Otherwise, any of your neighbours could use your broadband connection without your knowledge. Apart from wasting your bandwidth, this could also get you into trouble: if someone else uses your connection to do something naughty, the authorities will come knocking on your door rather than theirs.

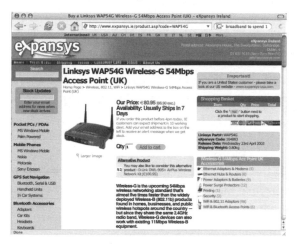

Buying a Wi-Fi access point at www.expansys.ie

To avoid this make sure to enable 'Wireless Protected Access' or WPA on your access point and laptop. Check the documentation that came with your access point for details on how to do this. If you got your access point from your ISP, they should be able to talk you through this. Otherwise, ask a tech-savvy friend to help you out, since a Wi-Fi access point can be fiddly to set up. See page 37 for suggestions on getting technical help.

Satellite

Broadband connections using satellite technology have been available for some time. These use a small satellite dish mounted on your roof to receive a broadband connection from an orbiting satellite. The advantage of satellite broadband is that it's available all over the country, even if you don't have (or can't get) a decent phone line. The disadvantages are:

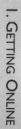

- It's usually more expensive than other forms of broadband, with per-minute or download fees in addition to the monthly cost.
- It needs a satellite dish and other equipment that can be costly to install.
- Although it will work reasonably well for browsing web pages, the delay on the satellite link will make some things, like interactive applications or voice chat, frustratingly slow.

Because of these limitations, I usually consider satellite connections only as a last resort if no other form of broadband is available.

Compare the options
The table below compares the main features of the different ways you can access the internet. Some details will change depending on your ISP, so check with them.

	Dial-up	ISDN	DSL	Fixed Wireless	Cable	Leased Line	Public Wi-Fi	Satellite
Always on	No	Yes	Yes	Yes	Yes	Yes	No	Yes
Per-minute charge	Yes	Yes	No	No	No	No	Depends on the location	No
Download speed in kbps	44	64 or 128	From 1,024 to 4,096	From 512 to 4,096	From 512 to 4,096	From 64 to 100,000 or more	From 512 to 4,096	From 512 to 2,048
What hardware do you need	Modem	ISDN terminal adaptor	DSL modem	Wireless antenna	Modem	Router	Wi-Fi card	Satellite dish
How to get hardware	Usually included with computer; otherwise €40	€75 – ask you ISP	Often free from ISP; otherwise €50	Comes from ISP	Comes from ISP	Costs from €800	Built into new laptops (Centrino or Apple); otherwise €35	Comes from ISP

CHOOSING THE CONNECTION FOR YOU

So, how do you choose which type of connection is right for you? Here are some guidelines to help you decide.

Starting off

When you're first going online, don't worry too much about getting broadband right away, and try not to get tied into a long contract with your ISP. Use a free, no-commitment dial-up service from eircom, British Telecom or one of the other ISPs while you get your feet wet. Take a couple of months to figure out how much you actually use the Net, and at what times of the day.

Once you are used to being online, consider getting a broadband connection. You'll be surprised how much broadband changes your internet use: everything happens a lot faster, so you can download music and watch video clips online without waiting around for it to download. Also, if you have a flat-rate plan you can stop worrying about how long you've been online so you end up using the internet a bit more.

To choose between a flat-rate dial-up package and the various types of broadband, find out what's available in your area and to your house. For example, you can call a couple of the DSL providers listed below and ask them to 'prequal' your phone line, which means they check whether it can support DSL. Also, call your cable TV provider and find out if you can get cable broadband in your house.

To choose between the different types of broadband, you can use the following rough rule of thumb: choose cable over DSL, and DSL over fixed wireless – but bear in mind that developments in the broadband market, as well as special offers, can change this.

If you can't get some type of broadband, or if you use the internet very little or just for email, keep track of how many hours you use the internet for a couple of weeks. This can help you decide whether a fixed-rate dial-up package is worthwhile for you – it usually is if you use the internet for more than fifteen evening and weekend hours per week.

Speeding up your connection

If you can't (or don't want to) get a broadband connection, you can try speeding up your dial-up connection with special software that compresses the web pages you're viewing. It won't perform miracles, but you might be able to squeeze a bit more speed out of a slow connection. There's usually a monthly fee to use this software, which is separate to any ISP costs. Check out www.onspeed.ie for one such service.

Download limits

Most broadband ISPs (including many DSL, cable, fixed wireless and satellite ISPs) will set a monthly *download cap*, sometimes called a *download quota* or *download allowance*. This is the amount of data that you can download each month on your broadband connection. The reason for this limit is to stop people swamping the ISP's network by downloading huge movies or pirated software twenty-four hours a day. This limit is usually set high enough that a normal user will never approach it. Common values are between 2GB and 8GB for most DSL connections (an 8GB cap is equivalent to downloading 5,000 copies of this book in a month). Some ISPs will also set an *upload cap*, which is the amount of data you can send out to the internet each month. Although you should never hit these caps through normal use, your ISP usually reserves the right to charge you more if you do go over them.

☞ Download quota examples: how many songs could you download a month with the following download limits?

2G limit	400 songs
4G limit	800 songs
8G limit	1,600 songs

CHOOSING AN ISP

When you're choosing your Internet Service Provider (ISP), it helps to have a good idea of what type of connection and package you want. See the previous sections for help on figuring this out. Then check the press for details of any special offers that are available. Call a few of the ISPs listed below and ask them what deals they have on at the moment (free installation, free modem, etc.). Don't let them talk you into signing up for anything right away, even a free trial (some of the 'free trials' can be surprisingly hard to get rid of!). Make sure to ask them these ten questions:

☞ **10 questions to ask your ISP**

- What installation fees will apply?
- Do I need any extra equipment (e.g. a modem) or is that included in the price?
- How long will it take to get connected?
- What monthly fees apply?
- Is there any limit to how much data I can download?
- Are there any other charges I might incur, like per-minute fees or download cap fees?
- When is technical support available (8 a.m.–8 p.m.? Twenty-four hours a day?)
- How much does it cost to ring the support line? (Some services use premium rate numbers.)
- Will this affect my phone service?
- How long is the contract? What if I want to terminate earlier?

Although that sounds like a lot of information, those are the questions you need to ask to make an informed comparison between ISPs. After all, you don't necessarily want to save a couple of euro a month on your subscription but end up paying more than that to ring the premium rate technical support number.

You should also check that your ISP is connected to INEX (the Internet Neutral EXchange), a switching centre in Dublin where Irish ISPs connect to each other. If your ISP has access to INEX, you'll have faster access to Irish sites.

While special offers can be attractive, make sure to evaluate the complete package. For example, don't be fooled by a free month's service if you're then locked into a one-year contract at a high rate. Remember that competition in the broadband market is heating up so you might want to switch ISPs in a few months.

☞ Some ISPs will quote a **contention ratio** for their service, usually expressed as a ratio, like '4:1' or '14:1'. This is supposed to indicate how much you'll be sharing the ISP's network with other users. For example, 4:1 contention is often touted as being twice as good as an 8:1 contention ratio. Some ISPs even claim to have 'uncontended' networks.

As neat as this sounds, unfortunately ISPs can (and do) twist, turn and manipulate these numbers for marketing purposes. Unless you have the time and inclination to understand how contention works on every single part of the ISP's network, I would ignore these ratios completely. They rarely mean anything.

Irish ISPS

These are the major ISPs in Ireland that, at time of writing, offer products for home users:

British Telecom   *www.btireland.ie*   *1800 923 923*
Good ISP for dial-up and DSL products. BT can be cheaper than eircom for some services.

Clearwire   *www.clearwire.ie*   *1800 882 333*
American company Clearwire has launched fixed wireless services in major Irish cities.

Digiweb   *www.digiweb.ie*   *1800 28 58 28*
Digiweb is best known for providing satellite broadband services throughout Ireland, but now offers a range of DSL services as well as good-value fixed wireless connections in many cities.

eircom.net   *www.eircom.net*   *1800 203 204*
eircom.net offers the full range of dial-up and DSL products.

Broadband options at www.digiweb.ie

Imagine   *www.imagine.ie*   **1890 92 92 92**
A relative newcomer to the DSL world, but they have competitive pricing.

Irish Broadband   *www.irishbroadband.ie* **1890 56 44 56**
Irish Broadband concentrate on fixed wireless connections in many urban areas in Ireland; they have packages for home users and businesses.

Leap/Magnet Networks *www.leap.ie*   **01 6114430**
Originally a fixed wireless provider concentrating on business users, Leap and Magnet now offer a range of DSL and fixed wireless products, as well as bundles of phone, TV and internet services in some areas. Pricing for their bundles is expected to be very competitive once they roll out in more areas.

Netsource   *www.netsource.ie*   **01 4336000**
Mainly deals with small businesses, but has some decent DSL products for home users looking for high-end services.

Smart Telecom   *www.smarttelecom.ie* **1800 718 555**
Smart Telecom were originally a discount phone call company but they have some great deals on DSL if you switch to their phone service too.

UTV Internet   www.utv.ie/internet

UTV have been providing internet service in Northern Ireland and the Republic of Ireland for some time and generally have competitive prices – and they don't charge a premium for technical support.

Cable Providers

Cable broadband is a great option if you can get it, but you're dependant on your existing cable provider offering the service in your area. The main Irish cable providers are:

Chorus   www.chorus.ie   1890 20 20 29

The major provider of cable TV outside Dublin; they offer broadband in some cities.

NTL   www.ntl.ie   1800 321 321

Previously known as CableLink, and soon to be renamed again.

Some new housing estates have their cable service provided by local companies who do exclusive deals with the developers. You'll have to ring them to see if you can get cable broadband from them. Their products vary in availability, price and performance. Make sure to ask them the ten questions for ISPs listed on page 33.

Wi-Fi ISPs

The Wi-Fi ISPs below provide services in public locations around Ireland. See their web sites for a list of hotspots where they provide service.

Bitbuzz (www.bitbuzz.com) 1850 BITBUZZ   1850 248 289
British Telecom (www.openzone.ie)   1800 924 924
eircom (www.eircom.ie)   1800 512 128
O2 (www.o2.ie)   1800 200 016
Vodafone (www.vodafone.ie/business/wifi)   1800 308 020

Wi-fi services on
www.bitbuzz.com

GETTING HELP

No matter how helpful your ISP is, sometimes connecting to the internet for the first time, upgrading to broadband, or publishing your web site can be tricky even when the engineer is at the end of the phone. It can be quicker and easier to find someone to help you onsite in your home or office. This can be especially useful if your computer has a virus that you can't remove.

It's often tempting to ask a computer-literate friend or relative to help you out, and this can be a great solution if you know someone tech-savvy. However, keep in mind that many computer professionals get hounded regularly by friends who can't get their email to work, or think they have a computer virus, or have another computer-related problem (a particularly beleaguered friend of mine has a t-shirt that says 'No, I won't fix your computer').

Although many people are happy to help, keep in mind that professionals sometimes become weary of being asked for free help and advice; you wouldn't expect a doctor friend to perform surgery for free, and you shouldn't expect a computer-literate friend to give up a lot of their time for nothing either. The offer of a tasty treat or a six-pack of beer will often work wonders in these circumstances!

If you don't know anyone you can ask for help, or if you need a lot of assistance with your computer and internet problems, it can often be worth turning to professionals. The firms below offer computer repair services and most will quote for a callout on request.

ACC Computer   *www.acccomputer.com*   *087 6660953*
Raheny, Dublin

Delamon IT Services *www.delamon.com*   *086 3354321*
Sandyford, Dublin

Motherboard   *www.motherboard.ie* *01 4975562*
Harolds Cross, Dublin

MTBS   *www.mtbs.eu.com*   *021 4273758*
Penrose Wharf, Cork

PC Ireland   *www.pcireland.com*   *086 125 4170*
Penrose Wharf, Cork

TechStore   *www.techstore.ie*   *1850 50 30 50*
Maynooth, Co Kildare.

Most of these only operate in a particular geographical area. To find a local supplier, check under 'Computer Maintenance and Repairs' in the *Golden Pages*.

If you're already online, you can also post a message on an online message board such as www.boards.ie (see page 87 for details on using message boards).

READY TO CONNECT

Depending on which connection you have chosen, before you can browse the web you may need to manually connect to the internet. If you have broadband, your computer is usually permanently connected to the internet. (Some broadband connections do need you to run a program to connect to them; check with your ISP if you're not sure.)

Dialling up

If you use a dial-up connection, you need to get your computer to **dial up** before you can browse. First, make sure your computer is connected to your phone line. A phone cable should have come with your computer or modem for this. It plugs into your modem at one end, and into your phone socket at the other.

Next, find the icon for your internet connection – your ISP's installation software will usually put this icon on your desktop.

The dial-up icon on a Windows desktop

If it's not there, go to My Computer/Control Panels/Network Connections and look for the icon there. Once you've found the icon, double-click on it to open the network connection box. Your username and password should already be filled in; just click 'Connect' to start the dial-up process.

If you're using a Mac, go to the icon of a phone in your menu bar, and make sure there's a tick by the name of your ISP. Then select 'Connect'.

Dialling up with a Mac

If the phone icon doesn't appear in your menu bar, you can find the Internet Connect program by opening Macintosh HD and clicking on Applications. Open Internet Connect by double-clicking on it, then click the icon for your modem (usually 'Internal Modem') and then click 'Connect'.

If you use a dial-up connection, or any connection where you're charged by the minute, make sure to disconnect once you're finished using the internet, otherwise you might get a nasty surprise on your next phone bill. Most broadband connections are 'always on' so you don't need to worry about disconnecting, but some are limited to a certain number of 'free' minutes each month, after which you're charged by the minute.

To disconnect, find the icon for your dial-up connection in the toolbar at the bottom of the screen. Right-click on the icon and choose 'Disconnect'.

On a Mac, go to the phone icon in your menu bar and select 'Disconnect'. If the icon doesn't appear, open Internet Connect, select your modem and click 'Disconnect'.

4. SOFTWARE

Once you're connected to the internet, you'll want to check out some web sites – that's where all the fun is! To access the **world wide web** (usually called 'the web'), you use a program on your computer called a **web browser**. This software allows you to connect to web sites and 'browse' them while you're online.

To start browsing, you need to launch your web browser. You do this by double-clicking on its icon.

YOUR WEB BROWSER
There are a few different web browsers available; they all do the same thing but with some small differences:

Microsoft Internet Explorer
If you have a Windows PC, Internet Explorer comes preinstalled on your computer. You'll find it either in the 'Start/Programs' menu or else right on your desktop, with a blue icon that looks like a large 'e'.

The Internet Explorer icon

Internet Explorer is handy because it's probably already on your computer, but it's also more prone to security problems than other browsers like Firefox (see below). Using Internet Explorer is fine to start with, but consider switching to Firefox later.

Safari

If you have a Mac computer, it probably came with Safari already loaded and in the Dock (the icons along the bottom of your Mac's screen). Safari is good and quite secure, but some web sites don't work properly with it. It's also not as fast as Firefox for some sites.

Firefox

Firefox is a free web browser that you can download from www.getfirefox.com. Because it's fast, secure and easy to use, I recommend installing it once you're up and running on the web and have mastered the basics. Installation is easy and free and is described in detail on page 129.

I. GETTING ONLINE

Chapter Two

THE BASICS OF WEB BROWSING AND EMAIL

1. WEB BROWSING BASICS

WEB ADDRESSES

When you open your web browser first, it will go to what's called your **home page** or **start page**. This is often set to the Microsoft web site, or the Firefox home page. Don't worry, we'll see how to change this later.

Every web site has an address (known as a '**URL**' or 'Universal Resource Locator') which you can use to access the page. Web addresses have this form: www.internetguide.ie

You might see the letters http:// in front of web addresses sometimes. You don't need to use these, since your web browser will add them automatically. Let's look at the format of a web address, e.g. http://www.internetguide.ie/hello

http:// This means it's a web page. If it's not included, your web browser will put it in for you.

www. Most web addresses start with 'www', which stands for 'world wide web'. (It's not very convenient: the acronym 'www' takes longer to say than the full words!)

internetguide.ie This is called the 'domain', and usually identifies the person or company that hosts the web site.

/hello This is the 'path', which shows which part of the web site you want to see. If it's not included, you see the main page of the web site.

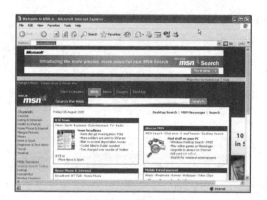

NAVIGATING THE WEB

Visiting a web site

If you know the address of a web site you want to visit, it's easy. At the top of your web browser window, there's a box which you can type into called an **Address bar**. If there's something already in the address bar, you need to clear that first. Click once in the address bar to highlight what's in it, then type backspace to delete it. Now type the web address you want to visit into the address bar and hit the Return key to go to that address.

This is handy if you read a web address in a newspaper, or someone gives it to you. For example, to access the web page for this book, put www.internetguide.ie into the address bar and hit Return. After a couple of seconds, the page should start to load. It can take a page thirty seconds or more to load and display fully, especially if there are lots of pictures in it, or if your connection is slow.

☞ When you're using web addresses, remember these tips:
• There are no spaces in a web address.
• The site name (www and the domain) is usually written in lower case (e.g. www.bitbuzz.com).
• The 'path' is case sensitive, so www.internetguide.ie/Hello is not the same as www.internetguide.ie/hello

Using Links

Once you're on a web page, you'll see that some of the words are underlined or in a different colour. When you move your mouse over them, the pointer turns into a hand. These are known as **hyperlinks** or simply **links**.

Links on
www.cnn.com

Clicking once on a link takes you to a different page (no need to double-click things on the web). This could be another part of the same web site or even an entirely different web site.

Clicking on links is the usual way to navigate through the web. Any part of the web page, including pictures, 'icons' and full sentences can be links. Try clicking on a few links and see where they take you!

Back and Forwards

If you click on a link and you want to go back to the previous page, just click on the 'Back' button in your web browser. That always takes you to the page you just left. Similarly, clicking the 'Forwards' button takes you to the link you had clicked on before clicking 'Back'.

Lost?

Some people are nervous about clicking links when they first go online, in case they get lost. Don't worry about finding your way

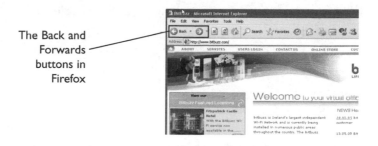

The Back and Forwards buttons in Firefox

back: you can always go back to the web address you started with by typing it into the address bar and hitting Return again.

Progress Bar

Once you type in a web address or click on a link it may take several seconds for the new page to load. This is usually based on the speed of your internet connection, although some sites get overloaded and are slow at times too. You can tell that the page is still loading by looking for the progress bar at the bottom of the screen in Internet Explorer and Firefox. This shows how much of the page is loaded.

The Progress bar in Internet Explorer

Searching the Web

What happens if you don't know the web address you want? You use something called a **search engine**. A search engine is a web site that acts like a searchable *Golden Pages* for the web; you just type in what you're looking for and it shows you a list of web sites that match. For example, you can search for 'RTE TV schedules' or 'pizza delivery in Galway' or 'Luas timetables'.

The most popular search engine is called Google, and it is available at www.google.ie. It's fast, free and quite comprehensive. Try visiting Google by typing its address (www.google.ie) into your address bar, and hit Return. Once you're there, type your query into the rectangular search box and click 'Google Search'. Google will respond with a list of matching pages; simply click the link to visit them.

Using Google well is something of an art form and I'll talk about it in more detail at the end of this chapter.

Setting your Start Page

Once you've used the web for a while, you'll probably find that there's a page you visit each time you're online. This might be a news web site (see page 145), or your webmail site (see page 50), or Google. For convenience, you can set your browser to automatically open this page when it starts. This type of page is known as your **home page** or **start page**.

To set your start page in Internet Explorer, go to Tools, select 'Internet Options' and make sure that the 'General' tab is selected at the top of the screen. Then type the address you want to use into the 'Address' box at the top. You can also click 'Use Current' to use the currently displayed web page.

Setting your start page in Internet Explorer

In Firefox and Safari, go to 'Preferences', click 'General' and fill in the 'Home page' box.

Once you've set a home page, you can click on the Home button at the top of the screen to go to that page at any time.

Bookmarks

If you're like me, you'll find a few sites that you visit regularly. Rather than having to type in their addresses each time you want to look them up, you can create a **bookmark** (also called a **favourite**) for the site. A bookmark puts the site's name in your web browser's Bookmarks or Favourites menu – just select it from the menu to open the site.

To create a bookmark, open the page you want to bookmark by typing its URL into the browser's address bar and hitting Return. Once the page is open, save your bookmark as follows:

- If you use Firefox, go to the Bookmarks menu and choose 'Bookmark This Page', then click 'Add'.
- If you use Internet Explorer, go to the Favourites menu and select 'Add to Favourites', then click 'OK'.

Your new bookmark will appear at the bottom of the menu. Now you can just select it from the menu to go straight to that site.

To delete or rename bookmarks, go to the Favourites menu and select 'Organise Favourites' in Internet Explorer. If you use Firefox, go to the Bookmarks menu and select 'Manage Book-marks'.

Adding a bookmark in Internet Explorer

Using Web Forms

On many internet sites you'll be asked to input information into your web browser. For example, you may need to register to use some features of the site, or you may be entering your billing details for online shopping. A web page where you input information is called a **web form**.

Using a web form is quite straightforward. There are a few different things you might see on a form that you're filling in:

Please enter your name:

A text input box. You can click in this box and type text into it.

☐ Yes, I would like a free sample.

A checkbox. Click the box to put a tick in it or remove the tick.

Please select your hair colour: Blonde ▾
Blonde
Brown
Red
Other

A drop-down menu. Click the arrow to see the available choices, and select the appropriate one.

Submit

A submit button. You click this when you're ready to send the form to the web server. The button can contain different text, but it will usually be easily recognisable.

When you're using a web form, remember that you're sending information across the internet. If it's sensitive information (like your credit card number or your *real* age), make sure to read page 70 on secure web sites.

2. EMAIL

The internet is full of things to do: shop, play, search, watch movies and listen to music. But the number one reason people get connected is to send electronic mail, or 'email'. Email is rapidly replacing conventional post for everyday business transactions (internet users sometimes call the post 'snail mail' due to its slowness). If you have friends or relatives living or travelling abroad, nothing beats email for staying in touch. It's fast, easy and (apart from the connection) free.

ANATOMY OF AN EMAIL ADDRESS

An email address uniquely identifies each person who sends or receives an email, like a postal address does for 'snail mail'. An email address has three parts:

The user name. This is generally some derivation of the person's name, like 'john' or 'johnsmith'. People's names are often separated with full stops, as in 'john.smith', pronounced 'John dot Smith'. Businesses also use generic user names like 'sales' or 'info'.

The @ symbol, pronounced 'at'. This separates the user name from the domain part.

The domain. This identifies the company the address belongs to. Some companies have their own domains, like 'mercierpress.ie' or 'kennys.com'. Some people use domains belonging to email providers like Hotmail, so their email domain will be 'hotmail.com'. Domains usually have two or three parts, ending in '.com', '.ie', or something similar. Each country has its own two-letter domain suffix, so someone in Italy might have an email address ending in '.it'. The '.com' suffix is used worldwide.

☞ alex	@	internetguide.ie
(user name)	('at' symbol)	(the domain)

49

Some important things about an email address:

You can't have a space in an email address. Use a dot instead. Usually, only letters, numbers, dots and hyphens (-) are used. Accents like fadas, apostrophes (') and strange characters confuse some computers and aren't allowed in email addresses (some people do have apostrophes in their addresses but these don't work on all computers, so should be avoided).

In email addresses, upper-case and lower-case letters are treated the same, so Alex@INTERNETGUIDE.ie is the same as alex@internetguide.ie.

What's my address?

So, now you know what an email address looks like, how do you get one? If you have email in work, your address will be assigned by your IT staff. Work addresses usually use a format like first name.lastname@company.ie.

For home use, your ISP will often give you an email address. For example, if you have a broadband connection from eircom, they will give you an email address ending in @eircom.net. You can usually pick the user name part, subject to the rules above, when you sign up. If you want to use the email address your ISP gives you, you usually need software on your computer called a 'POP email client' to download and read your email. Page 59 tells you how to use common POP email clients like Outlook or Eudora.

Your other option is to get a free web-based email account. This type provides you with an email address that isn't linked to your ISP, which means you don't have to change your address if you change ISP. You can also access your email from anywhere without any special software – you just use your web browser. See below to find out how to sign up for a free web-based email account with Yahoo! mail.

Getting a web-based email account address is the easiest way to get started with email. You can sign up for one or more free web-based email accounts, even if your ISP gave you an email address. You should also remember that you'll probably change your ISP at some stage, but you don't want to change email address if you can help it, so a web-based address is good to have.

☞ **Free web-based email services**
- **mail.yahoo.ie** Good free service from Yahoo!, with lots of features.
- **www.hotmail.com** The original free email service, now run by Microsoft.
- **www.gmail.com** Free email service from Google. Offers the best range of features and storage space. Not yet available to everyone though.

Yahoo! Mail

Signing up for a free email address is easy. Here we'll use Yahoo! mail as an example, but the process is similar with all of them.

To get started, go to mail.yahoo.ie. Here you'll be given the option to log in, or sign up for a Yahoo! ID. To use Yahoo! mail, you need to sign up for an ID, so select this option, then read and agree to the Yahoo! terms of service to continue.

Registering for mail.yahoo.ie

On the next page, Yahoo! asks you to enter some personal information to register for a free account. The boxes with the star next to them must be filled in to register.

☞ **Zip codes**

Many web sites assume you're in the US and expect you to have a 'Zip code' or 'postal code'. If the site won't accept a blank entry, try '99999' or '12345'

If you're wondering what Yahoo! will do with the information you provide, you can click on their 'Privacy Policy' right at the bottom of the page. See page 120 for more information about how web sites use your information.

The most important part of this form is the selection of your Yahoo! ID. This will also be the first part of your email address, with '@yahoo.com' after it. Since Yahoo! mail has been around for several years, most common names have been taken. Try putting your chosen ID into the Yahoo! ID box and clicking the button to check whether it's available. (Remember the rules about the format of email addresses on page 50.)

Pick your ID on mail.yahoo.ie

Yahoo! will open a small window telling you whether this ID is available. You may have to try a few different IDs to find one that you like and that's not taken. Here are some hints for finding an available ID:

- Try adding a number or year after your name, like 'jane2006' or 'mark123'.
- Try including a place name in your ID, like 'fiona_cork'.

- Sometimes a combination of your first and last names may be available, like 'john_smith' or 'smith_john'.
- You may need to combine a couple of the ideas above, for example 'marysmith2005' or 'johndublin1'.

After you've chosen your ID, fill in the rest of the registration page. This includes some questions you'll be asked if you forget your password.

Verifying that you're a real person on mail.yahoo.ie

Finally, many web sites ask you to copy a bunch of distorted letters and numbers into a box. This is to ensure that you're a real person, and not an automated program trying to register with the site. It can take a couple of tries to get this right.

YOUR MAILBOX

Once you've successfully completed the registration form, you'll be taken to your mailbox. Click on 'Inbox' to get started. The main things to notice on this page are:

- The list of messages in your inbox. Messages that you haven't read yet are shown in **bold**.
- Next to each message you can see the subject (short description) of the message, and the date it was sent.
- There are various buttons above the message list that you can use to do things with the message; we'll see what they do later.
- A list of 'folders' on the left-hand side. Folders are discussed more on page 57.

Reading messages

When you sign up for Yahoo! mail, they send you a welcome message, which appears in your inbox. To view a message, click once on the subject of the message (in this case, the word 'Yahoo!'). The full email message will appear.

An email inbox on mail.yahoo.ie

At the top of the email, you'll see the person who sent you the mail in the 'From' line, along with the message subject, when it was sent and what address it was sent to (your email address). These lines are often called the 'Message header'. Below the header you can see the email that Yahoo! sent you. You'll need to scroll down to see the entire message.

Above and below the message you'll see some buttons that you can use to do various things to the message. The most useful ones are:

Viewing an email on www.yahoo.ie

- 'Delete' will move the message into the 'Trash' folder, from where it will eventually be deleted completely.
- 'Reply' lets you send a reply to the sender of the message.
- 'Forward' sends on the email to someone else.
- 'Spam' tells Yahoo! that this message is an unsolicited ad, and should be deleted. Yahoo! will try and recognise messages like this as spam in future, too. See page 61 for more about dealing with spam.

Sending email

Sending an email works in the same basic way whether you use Yahoo!, Outlook or any other system. Remember, you need to have the email address of the person you're emailing. If you don't have one handy, send me an email; my address is:
alex@internetguide.ie

Composing an email at
www.yahoo.ie

- First, you select 'Compose' (or 'New message' on some systems).
- Next, fill in the email address of the person you're emailing in the 'To' box (remember, no spaces).
- Fill in a 'Subject' for the message. This is usually a one-line summary, like 'Your house is on fire' or 'Please call me about lunch'.
- Next, write the text of your email in the large box. Emails can be as long or as short as you like, but most are only a few paragraphs long. Remember to leave blank lines between paragraphs to make it easier to read.

55

- Finally, click 'Send' to send your email on its merry way.
- If you're not ready to send the email yet, most systems let you 'Save as a Draft' and come back to the email later.

☞ **Smilies**

Because it's often hard to convey the tone of an email properly, people use **emoticons**, also known as **smilies** to show emotions like humour in email. These look like faces if you turn your head to the left.

: -)   Happy, smiling or joking
; -)   Winking
: - (Frowning or sad
: - P Sticking out my tongue

You can see why smilies are useful if you consider the difference between these two sentences in an email:

I hate you.
I hate you : -)

Cost and speed

So, how long will your carefully crafted prose take to arrive? Usually emails get to the recipient within a few minutes of being sent. Sometimes they get delayed if the email has to go through complicated corporate networks or email filters. If your email takes a really long time to get through you usually get a warning message sent back to you telling you about the delay.

It's important to remember that sending or receiving an email doesn't cost you anything. You might be paying to be connected to the internet (see chapter one) but there's no extra cost for each message you send. So knock yourself out and email all your friends!

Using folders

Email systems give you a way to organise your email into different 'folders' for convenience. These are usually shown on the left-hand side of the email program. New emails will go into your inbox. When you send an email, a copy gets saved in your 'Sent' folder. Email that you delete is usually stored in the 'Trash'.

You can also create new folders to store messages; for example, you could create one called 'Work' for work-related emails, or one called 'Jokes' for funny emails you receive.

Using folders is useful once you start to get more and more emails. When you have a few dozen (or more) emails in your inbox it can be hard to find the exact one you want.

When you're viewing an email, you can move it to another folder. In Yahoo! mail, you use the 'Move' button to move a message into another folder. When you click Move, it shows you a list of available folders or lets you create a new one.

Sending attachments

Sending a few paragraphs of text back and forth is fine, but sometimes you want to send more interesting things, like pictures or documents. This is done by **attaching** a file from your computer to the email. It then gets sent along with the email as an **attachment**.

Attaching a file in Yahoo! mail

To send an attachment, compose your email as normal. Before you send it, click the 'Attach files' button in Yahoo! mail. In other systems, this button may be called 'Add Attachments' or may appear as a paperclip on the top of the email. Then click 'Browse' and an 'Open File' window will pop up. Find the file on your computer and click 'Open'. The name of the file will then appear.

Click 'Attach files' to send your file to the Yahoo! server (this may take a while if you have a slow connection or are sending a big file). Next, click 'Continue to message' and then send the message as normal.

Receiving attachments

When someone sends you an attachment in Yahoo! mail, a paperclip symbol appears next to the email.

Receiving an email
with an attachment
on Yahoo! mail

When you open the email and scroll down to the bottom of the screen, you'll have the option to 'Save to computer'. This downloads the file to your computer. In other systems, the attachment may be under the subject line of the email and you will be given the option to open the file or to save it somewhere on your computer.

Before you download any attachments, be sure to read about viruses on page 108. Viruses can use attachments to spread and infect your computer. Yahoo! mail will scan your email for viruses, but you should still have antivirus software installed on your computer.

Who's 'MAILER-DAEMON' and why is he emailing me?

If something goes wrong with your email, you'll usually get an automatic message advising you of the problem. These tend to originate from obscure email addresses like 'mailer-daemon' and

'Mail Delivery subsystem' and can be pretty confusing. These messages are known as 'bounces' (because they 'bounce back' when you send a message). The most common reason for receiving a 'bounce' is that you've misspelled someone's email address, so your message couldn't be delivered. The bounce will give you details of the error, and tell you whether your email has been rejected for some reason or just delayed.

Bounce messages from viruses

Sometimes you might get 'bounce' messages relating to emails you didn't send. If this happens, don't panic. Some virus software makes up email addresses and pretends to send email from those addresses. If you see these strange bounce messages, it means that a virus somewhere on the internet has randomly picked your email address to send messages 'from'; this does *not* mean that you have a virus, and you can safely ignore these bounces. They'll usually stop after a week or so.

Using an email client

If you want to use the email address your ISP gives you, you'll need to use a piece of software called a **POP3 email client**, often just referred to as an **email client**. The most common email client is Microsoft Outlook Express, which is pre-installed on most Windows computers and many Macs. Just as a web browser handles downloading and displaying web pages for you, your POP3 email client downloads and displays your email messages for you.

When you use a web-based email service like Yahoo! mail (see page 51), your email lives on the Yahoo! server. You view and reply to your messages through your web browser but Yahoo! stores the emails for you. When you use a POP3 email client, you download the emails to your own computer and remove them from your ISP's server.

Using the POP3 email client has a couple of important implications: first of all, if something happens to your computer, you may lose all your emails. Also, you can really only easily access your email from your own computer, using your email client (it is possible to access your mail in other ways, but they're not straight-forward).

Many people choose to use a mail client like Outlook Express because your ISP will provide instructions on setting this up. If you receive a software CD from your ISP, it will often configure Outlook Express for you automatically. Otherwise, call your ISP's support line and ask them to help you configure it. It's important that you get the settings from your own ISP since each ISP uses different settings.

To get started with Outlook Express, launch the program by double-clicking its icon on the desktop. If it's not on the desktop, find it by going to the Start menu and choosing 'Programs'.

Once you launch Outlook Express, you'll see the main wel-come window.

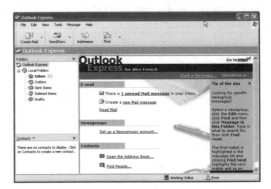

The Outlook Express welcome screen

Click on the inbox on the left-hand side to see the list of mes-sages waiting. Unlike a web-based email account, you need to tell Outlook Express to download any waiting email. Do this by click-ing the 'Send/Receive' button at the top of the screen. You need to be connected to the internet for this to work.

Most features of Outlook Express work in a very similar way to a web-based email account like Yahoo! mail. Read from page 53 for details on sending, replying and deleting emails, as well as working with folders.

To send a new message in Outlook Express, use the 'Create Mail' button. Remember that you need to click the 'Send/ Receive' button again to have Outlook Express actually send your email.

SPAM

Enhance your breast size! Get cheap medications! Make $$$ working from home! These are just some of the emails that drop into my inbox every day. They're all examples of Unsolicited Commercial Email (UCE), commonly called **spam**. The origins of the term 'spam' are lost in the mists of time, but it seems to have come from a Monty Python sketch.

The first spam was sent in 1978 (it was an ad for DEC computer equipment). For a long time, spam was a minor inconvenience, with some people receiving a few unwanted emails every week at most. But now, it's grown into a torrent of ads arriving in inboxes every day — I have one email address that receives over 250 pieces of spam each day.

A spam
email message

Spam works like this: spammers use sophisticated search programs to search through web pages for email addresses. They then send an email ad to hundreds of thousands, or even millions, of people. Since sending email is practically free, they make money if only a tiny fraction of people buy their product. Spamming has become a sophisticated industry, with specialists compiling and selling lists of email addresses and discovering ways to send emails which make them difficult to trace.

To try to combat spam, many email programs and services have built-in **spam filters**. These use complex rules to guess which emails are spam and filter them into a separate folder. Most spam filters let you 'train' them; you can mark particular messages as spam or not spam and the filters will improve their future results from this.

Spam filters are essential if you receive a large volume of spam, but they're not perfect. Some spam will always slip through. Also, be sure to regularly check the messages that have been flagged as spam. Most spam filters will occasionally give false positives, meaning that a 'real' message will occasionally get marked as spam.

Yahoo! mail and spam

I discussed setting up and using Yahoo! mail (mail.yahoo.ie) on page 51. Yahoo! mail has spam filters enabled by default. Anything Yahoo! thinks is spam gets moved to the folder called 'Bulk'. You can open this folder and read the messages like any other folder. If you see a message you don't think is spam, simply open the message and click the 'Not spam' button at the top. If Yahoo! missed a spam message, just click the 'Spam' button at the top of the email.

Dealing with spam

Spam filters and spammers are fighting a constant battle; as soon as a new type of spam comes out, someone writes a better spam filter, and so on. Apart from the technical battle, there are ongoing efforts to beef up legislation in the US (where most spammers are based) to allow state and federal governments to shut down and even imprison spammers. Although this would be a welcome move, the spammer would probably just move their operations overseas. Until we have better legal and technical tools to shut spammers down, they're here to stay. For a summary of spam history and antispam measures, both legal and technical, see www.templetons.com/brad/spam/.

To minimise the spam you get, you can take a couple of simple steps. First of all, if you have a web site of your own, or you post any information online, don't put your email address on the web pages. Spammers have automated tools that scan through web pages looking for email addresses. If you want people to contact you, try spelling out your email address like this:

alex at internet guide dot ie

rather than

alex@internetguide.ie

☞ **Tips for avoiding spam**
- Don't put your email address on a web page
- Never respond to spams: that just tells spammers that your email address is working
- Use an email system with a good spam filter, like Yahoo! Mail (mail.yahoo.ie).

Promoting products on the internet

Most ISPs take spam seriously, and will disconnect anyone caught sending spam. Because of this, you need to be very careful if you are going to use the internet to send out any sort of promotional material to customers or potential customers. Before you send out anything that could be considered unsolicited commercial email, take a look at www.spamfaq.net and read their 'Evils of Spam' document. The comprehensive internet document RFC 3098 (see www.faqs.org/rfcs/rfc3098.html) gives details on how to use the internet responsibly to promote products.

3. GOOGLE

The web has billions of pages of information; somewhere out there is a web page that will tell you how to build the perfect sandcastle; a site where you can buy a second-hand converted missile silo; and an awesome recipe for chocolate fudge brownies. All you need to do is find it.

As the web has grown, a lot of people have put a huge effort into helping us navigate all that information. Sites called **search engines** and **directories** try and organise sites and make it easy to find, say, the name of Henry the Eighth's third wife, or the time the next Luas leaves Sandyford.

The first big directory was Yahoo! (yes, they insist on spelling it with! an! exclamation! mark!). Yahoo! started by organising all the web sites they could find into different categories, like the *Golden Pages*. For example, suppose you wanted to find a site that would tell you how old you are, in seconds. On the Yahoo! home page you would click 'Science', then click 'Measurement and Units', then click 'Conversion', 'Online converters' and finally it would tell you that the site www.re-date.com can do what you need (my billion-second birthday is coming up soon!).

This way of finding sites, using a **web directory**, worked, but it was pretty slow and clunky. You can still use Yahoo! this way by going to the address dir.yahoo.com. Another good directory is www.dmoz.org, which is maintained by volunteer editors.

When it became obvious that directories wouldn't work as the web got bigger, the focus started turning to **search engine** sites. On a search engine site you type in simple words or phrases describing the page you're looking for. The search engine searches as much of the internet as it can and then shows you all the matching web pages that it can find – all in a couple of seconds.

There are a few search engines that you can use, and they're all pretty good. They differ in the details of how you use some features, and in the advanced features they provide, but all the ones listed below will help you find a good brownie recipe. Try them all (and any more you come across) and see which one you prefer.

A STEP-BY-STEP GUIDE TO USING GOOGLE

First, access Google by entering www.google.com into your URL bar and hitting Return. You can also use the address www.google.ie for the Irish version of the site, where you can choose to view it *as Gaeilge*. On Google.ie you can also select 'pages from Ireland' to restrict your search to Irish sites (this isn't 100 per cent accurate but does a reasonable job).

On the Google page, you'll see a 'search box' where you can type what you're looking for. Then click 'Google Search', or press return, to search.

Type what you're looking for

Then press 'Google search'

For example, imagine you're looking for that site that tells you how old you are in seconds. Entering the phrase 'age in seconds' and clicking 'Google Search' brings up a page like the one shown on the next page.

Google search results. Source: www.google.ie

Each section of the results page shows one web page that Google found that's relevant to your search words. For each one, Google shows the title of the page, a line or two from within the site, and the URL (address) of the site.

Online Conversion - How old are you?
Find out how old you are, and how long until your next birthday.
www.onlineconversion.com/howold.htm - 21k - Cached - Similar pages

Google search results. Source: www.google.ie

As you can see from the top of the page, Google found almost seven and a half million pages that sound relevant to the phrase 'age in seconds'. Google ranks them according to its best guess of what we're interested in, and shows them in order, best guess first. You can click on the title of a search result to go straight to that page. If you want to check out a different result, click 'Back' on your browser to return to the Google search results (see page 44 if you want a refresher on the 'Back' and 'Forward' buttons of your browser).

MAKING THE MOST OUT OF GOOGLE

Using Google can be something of an art, but it's well worth learning; with a bit of practice you'll be able to use it to unearth all sorts of stuff on the web. Here are some tips to get started:

Search terms

No matter how amazing Google can appear to be at finding obscure pieces of information in milliseconds, it's just a computer program, and can't read your mind – yet! If you want to get great search results, you have to give Google the right words to search for.

The first thing to remember is that some words are just too common to be useful in a search. Words like 'the', 'and', 'for' and 'a' appear in just about every web page on the Net and aren't much help in finding the page you want.

Also, keep in mind that many words can mean several things. For example, searching for 'soul' will give you results on soul food, soul music and selling your immortal soul. You need to include more words (like 'soul food recipes' or 'best soul albums') so that Google knows which kind of 'soul' you're interested in.

A great way to help Google find the right results is to think of other words that are likely to appear on pages that you're interested in. For example, if you're trying to find out what tennis racquet strings are made out of, including the word 'material' in your search helps to find more relevant results.

This example highlights something else you need to remember when you're searching online: a large proportion of the web is located in or designed for the US, so it can sometimes help to try spelling things the American way ('tennis racket string material' turns up a lot more results than spelling it 'racquet'; the same goes for words like 'color' rather than 'colour').

One last trick to keep in mind: usually, you just type words into the Google search box without any punctuation and Google looks for pages containing all of those words. Sometimes however, you want to find an exact phrase. To tell Google to find all your words *exactly as typed*, put double-quotes (") around the phrase. For example, searching for "Dublin pub guide" with the quotes will *only* find pages containing that exact phrase – and not pages about Cork pubs which happen to mention Dublin in them somewhere.

Other features

Google can also do some other neat stuff. Looking for a picture of Elton John? Click the 'Images' link above the search box to go to the Google Images search page, then enter 'Elton John' and click 'Search'. Google will search the web for images of, or related to, your search phrase. You'd be surprised at how many people turn up on Google Images, so try your own name or that of some friends to see if they're there.

I already mentioned that you can click on the option 'Pages from Ireland' to restrict your search (but only if you're on www.google.ie). You can also click on the button labelled 'I'm feeling lucky' rather than 'Google search'. This will take you directly to the top search result rather than showing a list of the results.

Similar pages

Google also gives a 'similar pages' link next to each search result. Clicking on this tells Google to analyse the page and find similar ones. This can be useful if one of the results is almost, but not quite, what you're looking for.

Excluding words

Sometimes, you want to tell Google to *exclude* pages containing certain words, by putting a minus sign '-' in front of them in the search box. For example, if you're looking for information on the Wimbledon area of England, searching for 'Wimbledon' will bring up mostly sites about the tennis open in Wimbledon. Searching for 'Wimbledon -tennis' will exclude tennis-related sites.

Excluding search terms on www.google.ie

Advanced Google searching

For most web searches, the main Google page provides plenty of functionality. If you really want to get down and dirty with advanced searching, you can click on the 'Advanced Search' link on the Google home page. This lets you specify more parameters for your search, such as pages in a specific language, or only pages updated recently.

Chapter Three

ADVANCED TOPICS
NEXT STEPS ON THE NET

1. ONLINE SHOPPING

Shopping online is one of the most underused features of the internet in Ireland. Although Ireland is high on the list of 'wired' countries, surveys consistently show that very few Irish people shop online. Although some people are (legitimately) worried about protecting their credit card numbers and personal information online, if you take a few basic precautions shopping online can be a really easy and efficient way to shop.

The sections below talk about some of the risks of shopping online, and the precautions you can take to reduce them.

RISKS AND PRECAUTIONS
Secure sites

In the early days of online shopping, people were worried that hackers could spy on their credit card details as they were sent over the internet. Although this isn't the biggest risk when you shop online, you should still check that any site where you submit personal details is a **secure site**. This means that data you send is encrypted to make it hard to spy on.

You can tell if a site is secure by looking for the icon of a lock at the bottom of your browser window. (They don't appear on all pages of the site.) You can double-click on the lock to find out details of the encryption between you and the web site.

Stored credit card numbers

A bigger risk when shopping online is what the merchant does with your credit card and other personal details once you submit

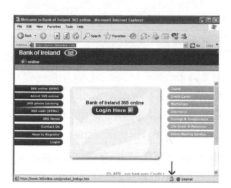

A secure web site,
www.365online.com

them. If someone breaks into their server, they could potentially find your credit card details. The only way to avoid this is to use reputable online merchants (see 'Common sense' below). After all, the same applies to a real shop!

'Secure shopping' guarantees

To reassure customers that online shopping is safe, some sites like Amazon.com provide their own Secure Shopping guarantees. They promise to reimburse you if your card is misused because you shopped with them. This can provide you with an additional layer of protection, but it's not usually necessary.

Viewing the security
details of a web site

Passwords and logging out

When you shop online or use services like eBay (see page 101) or PayPal (see page 104), you often register for an account with the web site. Make sure you don't give anyone else your password, or make it too easy to guess. If someone else can access your account on the site, they may be able to place an order in your name or even charge your credit card. It's more difficult to rescind a transaction if you gave someone else your password!

If you 'log in' to an online store or service, you should also be careful to 'log out' of each online store or service once you're done (there's usually a link on each page saying 'Log out' or 'Sign out'). Otherwise someone else using the computer after you may be able to access your account. This is especially important if you're using a public terminal such as a cybercafe.

VAT and Import Duty

When you buy from a retailer located outside the EU, your goods are technically liable for VAT and import duty when they arrive. This means that Irish customs can ask you to pay a fee before your goods are delivered. They usually won't bother for low-value items but you will often be asked to pay duty on cigarettes, alcohol or expensive electronics, sometimes even from inside the EU. Nevertheless, it can still be cheaper to order online and pay these fees than to buy things here, depending on the item.

Common sense

Before shopping online, check for real-world contact details (phone and address) for the merchant. That way, if something goes wrong you have an additional way to contact them. After any transaction, you should expect to get a receipt either on your screen or by email. If you don't, contact the merchant.

In general, you should treat an online shop the same way you would treat a bricks-and-mortar shop: if it looks suspicious, with no security and no contact information, don't go in!

YOUR RIGHTS
Fraud

When you use your credit card online, your card issuer (i.e. your bank) provides you with protection against fraud. In general, if you use your card responsibly, check your statements regularly and promptly report any suspicious transactions to your bank, you're not liable for anyone misusing your card. You may be asked to pay the first €10 or so (check with your bank for details) but by law you can't be held liable for more than €150. If you're worried about shopping online, this is your biggest safety net!

 Top tips for safe shopping online
- Make sure it's a secure site
- Check the site's contact information
- Find out about the merchant before you shop
- If it looks dodgy, don't go in!

Disputes

In this section we've been dealing mainly with fraud and credit card number theft, but what happens if you have a genuine dispute with the merchant? For online shopping within the EU, you have the same rights as if you bought something in a shop down the road. The Office of the Director of Consumer Affairs has an excellent web site giving you information on dealing with disputes. See www.odca.ie for details. The basic steps for disputing a transaction or dealing with fraud are:

1. If you find a suspicious transaction, try and contact the merchant directly to resolve the issue. Many merchants will quickly refund the transaction if they made a mistake.
2. If you can't get in touch with the merchant promptly, or if you are not happy with the results, contact your bank. Have the transaction reference, date and amount handy.
3. Be prepared to send your bank more details of the dispute, including documentation or emails you exchanged with the merchant.

Don't stress!

The risks above are real but rare. If you shop sensibly online and follow the Top Tips, you should be fine. And if something happens, your bank will usually not hold you liable. So get out there and shop! For top shopping sites on the Net, see chapter five.

2. ONLINE TRAVEL

CHEAP FARES AND GREAT CHOICE

Travel is one industry that has been completely transformed by the internet. Airlines and hotels used to pay travel agents commissions for handling their bookings, but with the internet everyone can be their own travel agent. Online bookings have almost completely supplanted traditional travel agents, and you can almost always save money by booking online directly with an airline or hotel.

The downside is that it can be laborious to find the best deal; for example if you want to find the cheapest flight to New York, you have try the Aer Lingus web site, the British Airways site, the BMI site, etc., since the best fares are only available on their own sites.

A good place to start is travel.yahoo.com, the Yahoo! Travel web site. Given a destination, it will give you a range of fares from different airlines. Just remember to try the airlines directly, too, since they'll usually have better deals.

The same is usually true of hotels: booking direct on a hotel's web site will generally save you money over using a travel agent. There are two exceptions though:

- Some travel sites, like Expedia (www.expedia.co.uk or www.expedia.com for the US site) will block-book rooms in popular hotels, and offer them online at a discount.
- As your travel dates get closer, some hotels will offer heavily discounted rates to fill empty rooms. These discounts can be significant – often fifty per cent off the original price.

Because of these factors, it's worth checking some of the main travel web sites for good hotel rates as well as checking directly with the hotel's site. Hey, it's free to check!

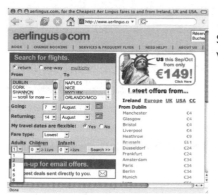

Selecting flight details on www.aerlingus.com

Booking a Flight

For most people, one of the first internet purchases they make is flights on www.ryanair.com or www.aerlingus.com. The process is similar for all airline sites: you select your starting point, destination and travel dates and you're given a list of fare options. On low-fares airline, the outbound and return flights are often priced separately, so remember that both fares will be added together at the end of the process. Also, some sites only add in the taxes and charges at the end of the process, so you have to finish selecting your flights before you see the actual price.

Once you've selected the flights, you pay online using a credit card. Most airlines also allow you to call them and give your credit card number over the phone, but there's usually a surcharge for this.

After you pay, you'll get a confirmation page. It's extremely important to keep a copy of the confirmation reference on this page. If possible, print the page out (you won't be able to come back to this page later). The web site should also automatically send you an email containing all of the confirmation details for your records. When you book online, you usually don't get a paper ticket sent to you in the post anymore. Instead, the airline uses what's called an 'e-ticket'. This means that you check in using your passport and a print-out of the confirmation details (usually the email that you were sent).

When you book air tickets or accommodation online, it's really important to check the details of your booking before you complete it. Because you're making the booking yourself, you can't blame anyone else for mistakes! Online airline bookings usually have more restrictions than bookings made through a travel agent. If you want to change the booking once it's made, you might have to pay a large surcharge. Some bookings are completely non-refundable and non-changeable, but others can be changed if you pay the difference between the new fare and the original one. Because the rules are different for each airline and even each type of ticket, read the small print carefully to make sure you know the conditions that apply to your booking.

If you're booking a hotel, look for the cancellation policy in the small print. Most hotel bookings can be cancelled up to 24 hours in advance with little or no penalty, but some heavily-discounted internet rates have to be paid in full at time of booking and are completely non-refundable.

TRAVEL BOOKING SITES
www.expedia.com (US) or www.expedia.co.uk (UK/Ire)
Be careful – Expedia.co.uk will only send tickets to a UK address for some bookings.

travel.yahoo.com
www.travelocity.com

Some useful airline web sites:
   www.aerlingus.com
   www.ryanair.com
   www.ba.com
   www.flybmi.com
   www.aerarann.ie

www.directski.com
This is an Irish site that provides low-cost ski and snowboarding holidays in Europe by dealing directly with the resorts rather

Making a booking on
www.aerarann.ie

Aer Arann — Book online at aerarann.com.194

http://www.aerarann.com/skylights/cgi-bin/skyligl

Search Select Summary Details Payment Itinerary

NEW DOMESTIC SECURITY CHANNEL AT DUBLIN AIRPORT
Aer Arann is delighted to announce the introduction of a new dedicated security channel for
domestic passengers traveling through Dublin Airport.

Here are the flights and fares available on the requested date(s). Fares do not include tax.
1. Please review the flights offered. Click a fare name to see fare rules & restrictions.
2. Click on a plane icon or accompanying dot to select your flight of choice.

Going Out

	O Fare Adult Regular € 44.99 EUR	Mon, 08 Aug 05 Flight 231	09:30 Depart Dublin (DUB) 10:15 Arrives Galway (GWY)
	P Fare Adult Regular € 76.99 EUR	Mon, 08 Aug 05 Flight 233	13:15 Depart Dublin (DUB) 14:00 Arrives Galway (GWY)
	M Fare Adult Regular € 71.99 EUR	Mon, 08 Aug 05 Flight 237	18:30 Depart Dublin (DUB) 19:15 Arrives Galway (GWY)
	V Fare Adult Regular € 34.99 EUR	Mon, 08 Aug 05 Flight 239	22:30 Depart Dublin (DUB) 23:15 Arrives Galway (GWY)

Coming Back

than going through a tour operator. They usually have fantastic last-minute trips available, too.

www.venere.com
Excellent site to help you pick a hotel in Europe, which includes reviews and ratings by other guests, maps and online booking. I've used this several times and it's great to see what other people think about hotels before you book.

www.flightview.com
Fun site that allows you to see the location, speed and heading of transatlantic flights in real time. Keep an eye on your friends while they're in the air!

www.clubtravel.ie
Good site for tracking flight prices from Dublin.

www.airlinemeals.net
Onboard meals on various airlines photographed and rated by passengers.

www.lastminute.ie
UK-based site that specialises in trips booked just a few days before. Some of the flights are UK-based, but the hotel deals can be fantastic!

www.sunway.ie
Good selection of package holidays, with discounts if you book online.

www.holidays-uncovered.co.uk
Reviews of popular resorts by real people! Find out what 'close to the beach' really means ...

www.frommers.com
Online edition of the global guidebooks – free. Some great suggested itineraries if you only have a couple of days in a city.

www.seatguru.com
A guide to the best (and worst) seats on different airplanes. Invaluable for long-haul trips.

www.rentalo.com
Good site for independent apartment rentals worldwide. Renting a self-catering apartment can be a great option but be sure to check the location and amenities.

www.fco.gov.uk/travel/
The UK Foreign Office list of warnings about travel and risks around the world. Check it out before you go anywhere too exotic.

www.tmb.ie
Check out what vaccinations you need for any exotic destinations (they may be a bit overzealous ... they recommend hepatitis vaccinations if you're headed for 'rural Ireland'). This site is also a good source of travel news and health information for most countries around the world.

www.explore.co.uk
UK-based travel agent specialising in group-based, guided activity tours. Perfect for single travellers.

www.homeexchange.com

Doing a house swap can be a cheap and interesting way to see faraway places. It can take a few months to organise, and you might want to lock up the Ming vases, but the internet is the perfect way to find a likeminded person to swap with. You'd be surprised how many people with amazing houses in Florida or apartments in Manhattan want to spend a week in an Irish house.

3. BUILDING YOUR OWN WEB SITE

So you've seen a bunch of other people's web sites ... and now you fancy having your own. Your own web site can be a great way to communicate with friends all over the world; share news and photos with your family; or promote a small business. If you're really ambitious, you can do lots more like host a discussion on your favourite topic, or sell products directly from your web site.

Choosing your page design on yahoo.com

HOW WEB SITES WORK

To start out, you need to understand a little about how web sites work. Every site, from my own site right up to Yahoo.com, uses a simple language called Hyper Text Markup Language, or HTML. HTML is used to specify what text goes on a page; what images go where; and which parts of a page link to other pages. To create a web site, you create HTML pages and put them on a web server. This server *hosts* the site and allows people to see your site twenty-four hours a day. To make things easier, there are a bunch of tools that you can use to build a web site. These create the HTML files for you, based on how you want your site to look.

Designing your page on yahoo.com

GET STARTED
Web site host

A good way to start out building your own site is to sign up with Yahoo!'s Geocities service. This lets you build a simple web site, which is hosted on Yahoo!'s server, for free. They place small ads on your site to pay for the service.

To build your site, go to geocities.yahoo.com. If you're not already registered with Yahoo!, you need to sign up for a Yahoo! ID (this is free). Once you're logged into Yahoo!, click on the 'Sign up' button under the 'Free Web Hosting' option. Follow the simple steps to register for the service. You'll then be told the address, or URL, of your own web site. It will be something like www.geocities.com/your_id

This is the address you'll give to people so that they can see your web site.

So now you have a web site (you can try typing its address into your URL bar to see it) ... but there's nothing there yet. To create pages for your site, you can use the simple tools that Yahoo! provides to help you, called 'wizards'. The PageWizards tool guides you through simple steps to create a one-page web site in under ten minutes.

If you want more flexibility, like uploading your own pictures and having multiple pages, try the PageBuilder tool. This is more powerful than PageWizards and gives you more control over how your pages look. PageBuilder also has some pre-built templates that you can choose from, like a 'Baby pictures' web site or a 'My Pet' site

Learning HTML

For ultimate flexibility, you'll need to learn some basics of HTML. This will give you more control of your web site. Even if you use a tool like Yahoo! PageBuilder, it's useful to have a basic knowledge of HTML, so you understand what's going on 'under the hood'.

There are lots of sites that will teach you about HTML. I like the W3 Schools HTML tutorial, at www.w3schools.com. This is a good intensive tutorial with lots of examples, and it's free. If you're going to be using HTML, I also recommend getting a good introductory book that you can use as a reference. My favourite is *Creating Web Pages* by Preston Gralla and Matt Brown which covers all the basic topics as well as some advanced ones.

If you create your own HTML pages, you first save them onto your computer, and then upload them to the server where they are hosted (for example, the Yahoo! server). You can get information on how to do this from the server's help pages.

HTML editors

To help you create your HTML pages, you can install an HTML editor. This is a program that lets you create web pages by dragging and dropping text and images. You can usually switch back and forth between seeing how the page will look, and the underlying HTML that will be uploaded to the server. Most HTML editors also make it easy to upload your pages to the server. A good free HTML editor is Mozilla Composer. You can download it from www.mozilla.org/products/ (look for 'Mozilla Suite'). There is a good guide to using Mozilla Composer available at www.thesitewizard.com/gettingstarted/mozillacomposer1.shtml

(this site also has lots more useful information about creating and publishing your web site).

Web sites and your ISP

Some Irish ISPs will give you space on their servers to host your web site at no extra cost. If you want to use this space, you need to create your own HTML pages, from scratch, or using an HTML editor (see above for information on how to do this). Your ISP should provide you with the URL for your web site (like www.netsource.ie/myname) as well as the setting you need to upload your site.

The advantage of using your ISP's webspace is that it's often free, and won't have any ads placed on it. The downside is that this webspace and its address (URL) is tied to your ISP, so if you ever change ISP you'll have to move your web site and change its address, which can be a chore.

Master of your own Domain

So far in these examples the address of your web site has always been dependent on the server where it's hosted, such as:

www.geocities.com/my_id

or

www.netsource.ie/myname

This is fine for a personal web site, but for a more professional look, you might want to consider registering your own 'domain'. This is the 'geocities.com' part of the address. Most businesses will register a specific domain name, so the address of their web site will be www.mycompany.com. For example, www.bitbuzz.com.

Domains can end in .com, .net, or a few other suffixes. Each country also has its own suffix; Ireland's is .ie. The cost of registering a domain name varies depending on your ISP and which suffix you want. .com domains are the easiest to get and also the cheapest, starting at €10–€50 per year. .ie domains are generally around €100 per year and require some paperwork to register. .ie domains generally have to be registered through an Irish ISP.

Unless you're an advanced internet user, the easiest way to get your own domain name is through your ISP. They'll take care of registering it on your behalf, providing the technical nuts and bolts (known as 'name service') and pointing the domain name at your web site. For example, if you already have a Yahoo! Geocities free site, you can upgrade it to a 'Pro' site, including your choice of .com domain name, for around €60 per year.

If you're setting up a new web site for your business, here are some service providers to check out. They provide various packages including hosting your site, registering your domain name and other features like online selling tools.

Hosting packages at www.hosting365.ie

domains.yahoo.com. Yahoo! has a full suite of products, from the free Geocities service all the way up to high-end high-performance services.

www.hosting365.ie Ireland's largest web site hosting company; good range of products, local support and competitive pricing.

www.novara.ie Another good Irish choice with a range of hosting products for small businesses.

4. BLOGGING

WHAT IS A BLOG?

A 'web log', or 'blog', is an online journal that anyone can read. People use blogs to communicate with friends and family; keep colleagues and customers updated on new projects; or engage in 'citizen journalism'. Since blogging started in 2002, millions of people have created their own blog, writing about whatever topics interest them. Blogs tend to be updated frequently, often daily, with small snippets of information.

Some blogs are mainly personal, intended for the author's friends to read; others are daily reports about a particular celebrity, a film genre, or the happening in a small town. Politicians have started keeping blogs to keep in touch with constituents more regularly and informally than traditional media can accommodate. Journalists often blog to give them flexibility to comment on breaking news without the formality of writing an entire article.

The huge explosion in blogs has led some people to speculate that blogging will take over from traditional forms of journalism.

☞ Blogging is a fun and easy way to keep relatives and friends up to date with your news. To see some blogs, try the sites below:

weirdweb.blogspot.com: My blog, where I post news about technology issues in Ireland, as well as interesting web sites that I find.

www.breakingnewsblog.com: A selection of blogs on a range of topics, each run by a different person, collected in one site for ease of browsing.

blogs.guardian.co.uk/news/: Even mainstream news sites have started using blogs ... the Guardian site lets journalists post breaking news throughout the day.

www.engadget.com: This hugely popular blog is my favourite source for technology and gadget news.

After a major new event, bloggers are often the first to provide breaking news on the internet. However, as with many things on the internet, you have to consider the source of any information carefully; as news bloggers often rush to post the latest information online, it may be less carefully vetted than traditional news sources.

Creating a blog on www.blogger.com

GET YOUR BLOG ON

If you're interested in starting your own blog, it's easy (and free). There are several sites that will let you create and manage a blog, but my favourite is Blogger, run by Google.

To create a blog, go to www.blogger.com and sign up for an account. You can pick a name for your blog, 'jims_blog', for example, which will then appear at the following address: jims_blog.blogspot. com.

You can give this address to friends, family and colleagues. Once you're signed up, you can go to the Blogger any time and add a new 'post', which will appear on your blog page.

Blogs are great for keeping people up-to-date, sharing information, or good, old-fashioned rants. A popular blog can quickly accumulate thousands of people who visit it regularly to hear the

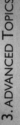

Writing a blog entry on www.blogger.com

latest about Tom Cruise's love life, your insight into Aston Villa's performance, etc.

A word of warning though: blogs are public, and you never know who might stumble across yours. Don't say anything in a blog that you wouldn't say in a public forum, or you might get into hot water. In the US, people have been fired for revealing confidential information about their workplace in a blog, and for using a blog to post derogatory information about colleagues. So enjoy blogging, but don't say anything that's libellous or will get you into trouble with work.

5. CHATTING ONLINE

Email is great for communicating with people ... as long as you know their email address, and don't mind waiting a while for the reply. Online chat takes internet communication to the next level, allowing you to type messages to individuals or groups of people. There are three types of online chat that we're going to cover in this section:

- Message boards
- Live chat rooms
- Instant messaging

☞ If you or your family are going to use any online chat features, be sure to read chapter four: protecting yourself online.

MESSAGE BOARDS

Internet message boards are web sites that let you write comments on a topic (known as **posting** a message) and see other people's replies (or **posts**). It's not quite live, since it may take a while for someone to post a reply, but busy topics can have dozens of posts throughout the day.

Post messages online on www.boards.ie

A nice site to visit if you want to see how message boards work is www.boards.ie. This Irish site has message boards covering topics from pets to alternative music, and everything in between.

Like many message boards, you can browse through the site and read other people's postings for free, and without having to register. If you want to reply or post your own message, you need to register for a free account. This lets the site **moderators** track postings and ban people who don't obey the site's rules or etiquette. On www.boards.ie, you can also associate a picture icon with your posts to identify them.

Why do people like message boards so much? Mainly because

they create a virtual community of people who are interested in similar topics. If you regularly read the Pets forum on www.boards.ie, you will begin to recognise and relate to the other people who post. Think of it as a big room where you can find other pet lovers at any time of the day or night! Many people end up developing friendships (both online and in the real world) with people they meet on message boards.

If you're interested in any of the topics or discussions on a message board, I recommend spending a few days simply reading other people's posts and learning the accepted rules of etiquette for that forum before you post. (Reading a message board without posting is known as **lurking** on the board.) Saying the wrong thing in the wrong way on a message board, like in any social situation, can give a bad first impression. For example, going on a Dublin GAA message board and saying 'Kerry is the best football team ever' is likely to elicit the wrath of the regulars and result in many nasty replies. This is known as **flaming** (because the discussion suddenly gets really hot) and can be avoided by judicious lurking before you post!

☞ **Common chat abbreviations**

BRB:	Be right back
FAQ:	Frequently Asked Questions
LOL:	Laughing out loud
IMHO:	In my humble opinion
a/s/l:	age/sex/location (i.e. 28/m/Dublin)
PM:	Private message (not seen by whole room)
FYI:	For your information
THX:	Thanks
ROTFL:	Rolling on the floor laughing
WB:	Welcome Back

For more, see familyinternet.about.com/od/ sharingonline/a/acronyms.htm

LIVE CHAT ROOMS

Live chat rooms let you communicate, live, to all the other people in the chat room. Anything you type appears on their screen and vice versa. This can often feel like shouting to people across a noisy pub; several conversations can be going on at once, and people join and leave the chat room constantly.

Chat rooms are often organised into different categories, like message boards. A good place to start is chat.yahoo.com, which has dozens of chat rooms to choose from. To use Yahoo! Chat, you need to register for a (free) Yahoo! account.

In chat rooms, people tend to use abbreviations to make typing easier and quicker. This can be confusing the first few times you see it. Don't be afraid to ask if you don't understand something.

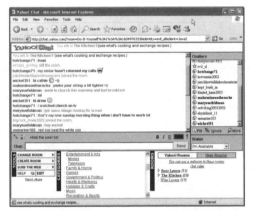

Chatting live on chat.yahoo.com

In Yahoo! Chat, a list of other people in the chat room appears on the right-hand side. The buttons under the list let you send a **private message** ('PM'); ignore a user (their comments no longer appear on your screen); or see more info on a user.

The bar along the bottom is where you type your message. Once you hit Return, it's sent to the server and will shortly appear in the main chat area.

Remember, live chat is essentially unmoderated (see page 123 for some exceptions) so the language can be colourful at times.

The moderators of each chat room have the ability to 'kick' anyone who doesn't stick to the rules of the room, though, and they aren't afraid to use it!

INSTANT MESSAGING

Instant messaging, commonly called **IM**, lets you type back and forth with one person or a small group. This is great for communicating with friends in another country; just arrange to be online at the same time and you can chat online practically for free (like email, there is no additional charge to use instant messaging; you are only paying for being online). IM is rapidly becoming a useful tool for businesses too, allowing people in different offices and even different countries to collaborate in real time. I've worked on several projects where the main method of communication between team members from different companies and time zones was through IM, with an occasional phone call thrown in.

To use instant messaging, you need to sign up for one of the IM systems (they're all free!). The main IM systems are:

- AOL Instant Messenger (AIM)   www.aim.com
- Yahoo! Messenger   messenger.yahoo.com
- ICQ   www.icq.com
- MSN Messenger   www.msn.com

They all provide similar functionality, but they don't interoperate. So if you sign up to AOL, you can only chat to other people who have signed up with AOL. If you know you want to chat to a specific person, ask them which system they use and go for that one.

(You can sign up for multiple IM systems if you want, but this gets confusing after a while since each needs it own software.)

To sign up with an IM system, you need to go to their web site and download a special piece of software called an 'IM client'. This is the software that you use to type messages to others and keep track of people you want to communicate with.

Once you have the software, you also need to sign up for an account with the IM system you've chosen (this is free). When you sign up, you need to pick an ID that allows others to find you. Like your email address, you'll need to give this to others so they can reach you.

Yahoo! messenger

Here's how to download and start using Yahoo! Messenger, but the process is similar for the other systems.

Go to messenger.yahoo.com and click on 'Get it now' or 'Download'. Follow the simple instructions on screen to download and install Yahoo! Messenger. You'll have to agree to Yahoo!'s terms and conditions and go through a couple of simple steps to install the program. Once it's installed, you'll be asked to launch the program and enter your Yahoo! ID (you can opt to register if you don't have one yet).

Using Yahoo! Messenger

Now that you have Yahoo! Messenger installed, it's time to start chatting. Before you can send an instant message to someone, you have to add them as a 'friend'. This is what Yahoo! Messenger calls someone you want to be able to exchange messages with; other IM systems also refer to this as a 'buddy'. To add a friend, click 'Add' and type their Yahoo! ID. You can also 'search for friends': this opens a web page where you can search by name, ID, or location. The most common way to get someone's ID is to ask them for it, by phone or by email.

Once you've added someone as a friend, their name appears in your friends list. It changes colour if they're also signed on to Yahoo! Messenger.

To send someone an IM, double-click on their ID. This opens a new window where you can type your message. If your friend is online, they will receive your message right away; otherwise, the message is stored and they receive it the next time they sign on to Yahoo! Messenger.

Unwanted chatters

On some IM systems, you can choose whether you want people who are *not* on your friends list to be able to send you messages. If you want to meet new people from other parts of the world, you might want to allow this, but it can get annoying to have random messages popping up on your screen from people you don't know!

☞ Parents should be especially careful of children using live chat rooms. Make sure to read the section on protecting your kids on page 121.

Yahoo! toolbar

Unless you tell it not to, Yahoo! Messenger also installs something called the Yahoo! Toolbar. This is a row of buttons that will appear at the top of your web browser window so that you can quickly access the Yahoo! site. If you want to get rid of this toolbar, just go to the View menu, select 'Toolbars' and un-tick 'Yahoo! Toolbar'.

6. ONLINE MUSIC

Whether you like Rachmaninov or Snoop Dogg, the internet is a great place to find, buy and listen to music.

This section will tell you all you need to know to start downloading music from the Net. For information on buying cheap CDs and tracking your favourite bands online, see the directory listings in chapter five.

THE LEGACY OF NAPSTER

You may have heard that downloading music from the internet is something illegal that people do under cover of darkness; that used to be true. In May 1999 a college student named Shawn Fanning wrote and released a program called Napster. It allowed people to share any music they had on their computers with anyone, anywhere, who also had installed Napster. Almost overnight, millions of users started illegally copying each others' music. At its peak in 2000, an average of 1.5 million users were connected to Napster *at any one time*, getting all the free music they wanted.

The music industry quickly realised the potential threat to CD sales that Napster posed and went to court to shut it down. By February 2001 Napster was ordered to start screening the files that were shared and the service was closed shortly after that.

Although Napster's service wasn't legal, its huge success showed the demand for downloading music. Several companies quickly started offering legal download services. The best of these is Apple's iTunes Music Store, which offers millions of songs that you can download for under €1 each. Complete albums cost under €10. (After its demise, Napster's name was purchased by another company and the software was relaunched as a legal music store, similar to iTunes. It's available at www.napster.com, although at time of writing Irish users can't sign up to it.)

☞ **File sharing:** There are other programs, like LimeWire and Kaazaa, that people still use to swap files and music, which are often of dubious legality. If you do decide to try one of these programs, keep in mind that you might be breaking the law if you grab a copyrighted file from someone else. You're also at an increased risk of getting a virus, so make sure you have antivirus software installed and running. See page 110 for details on antivirus software.

Get iTunes

To use the iTunes Music Store, you need to download and install the iTunes software. This manages your music library and lets you listen to your music and burn CDs. iTunes is available for Windows and Macintosh computers.

The iTunes main window

To download iTunes, go to www.apple.com/itunes and click the 'Download' button. When asked, save the file somewhere on your computer that's easy to find, like your desktop. After the download completes, double-click on the downloaded file to install iTunes.

Using iTunes

iTunes is a great tool for organising any music you have on your computer. You can click on an artist to see all the songs you have by them, or search for songs by typing a few letters of the name, album or artist.

Ripping CDs

iTunes makes it easy to copy your CDs into digital format (called 'ripping' the CD). Simply insert the CD into your CD-ROM drive and it will appear in iTunes. Click the 'Import' button to copy the songs to your computer. Ripping a CD to your computer takes around ten minutes.

> ☞ **Tip:** make sure you're connected to the internet when you insert a CD to be ripped: iTunes will automatically look up the names of each song and add them to your music library.

Using iTunes to rip a CD

Making playlists

Playlists let you organise your songs and listen to them in any order. To make a playlist, click the '+' button in the bottom left corner of the iTunes window. Type a name for it, then drag any tracks to the playlist. To listen to songs in your playlist, click its name and then the Play button.

> ☞ You can fit between ten to fifteen songs on an audio CD. iTunes will automatically split longer playlists across two or more CDs.

Burning CDs

If your computer has a CD writer in it you can create a CD from any of your playlists and listen to it in a normal CD player. (You can buy a CD writer in any good computer store for around €100).

To create a new CD (known as 'burning' the CD) you need a blank CD to put your music on. You can buy blank CDs in any music or stationery shop; look for ones labelled 'CDR' or 'CDRW'. If you want to play your CD in a normal CD player, check the following setting in iTunes: go to the 'Preferences' menu option, click 'Burning' and make sure that 'Disc Format' is set to 'Audio CD'.

CD burning preferences in iTunes

Now click on the playlist you want to make into a CD and click Burn Disc. iTunes will prompt you to insert a blank CD into the drive. That's all there is to it! Burning a CD takes up to half an hour depending on the speed of your CD drive.

iTunes Music Store

One of the coolest things about iTunes is the online music store, where you can buy and download over 1.5 million songs. To get started, make sure you're online and click the 'Music Store' icon in the left-hand window of iTunes.

You'll need to register for the iTunes music store and provide your credit card number to buy music (don't worry, you won't be charged unless you actually buy something). If you're not automatically asked to register, click the 'Sign In' button on the top right corner.

Sign up for the iTunes music store

Once you're signed into the iTunes store, you'll see the main page, showing the top-selling songs and albums. From here you can search or browse the entire collection of songs available to download.

The iTunes music store

Try clicking on a track or an album to see its details and pricing.

Viewing an album on the iTunes music store

☞ Try before you buy: you can double-click on a song to hear a short excerpt for free.

You can buy songs in one of two ways. With 'one-click' ordering, you just click 'Buy song' or 'Buy album' to purchase music. Your credit card gets charged and the song starts to download onto your computer.

Selecting a song in the iTunes music store

This is convenient, but you might end up impulse-buying a lot of music. I use 'shopping cart' buying instead. In this mode, you add music to a virtual 'shopping cart'. When you're done shopping, you click on your shopping cart and 'check out' to confirm your purchases. This gives you a chance to think twice about buying all the Westlife albums ever made.

You can change between 'one-click' and 'shopping cart' mode by going to the Preferences menu option in iTunes and selecting 'Store'.

The shopping cart
in iTunes

Choosing your shopping modes in iTunes

7. ONLINE AUCTIONS

Online auction houses have been bringing buyers and sellers to-gether for several years. Whether you're looking for a concert ticket or trying to get rid of junk from your attic, auctions can be a cheap and effective way of buying or selling online.

The best known auction site is eBay (www.ebay.ie) but Yahoo! also run an auction service (auctions.yahoo.com).

Auctions aren't just for antiques buffs anymore: over 125 mil-lion people do business on eBay every day, with over €1,000 of goods being sold *every second*. Thousands of people, mainly special-ised dealers, make their living using eBay to buy and sell goods. You can buy just about anything in an online auction these days, from a hard-to-find vinyl record to a house. eBay is mainly used for trading run-of-the-mill items, but bizarre items auctioned on eBay include the fingernails of serial killer Roy Norris ($9.99); a book on how to knit with dog hair ($8.99); someone's soul ($10.50); and 'nothing' (it didn't sell). A toasted cheese sandwich that looked like the Virgin Mary recently sold for €25,000 (no, I'm not making this up).

Using an online auction site is straightforward: first, you have to register and provide some proof of who you are, usually in the form of a credit card number. This helps to ensure that only legiti-mate buyers and sellers participate in an auction.

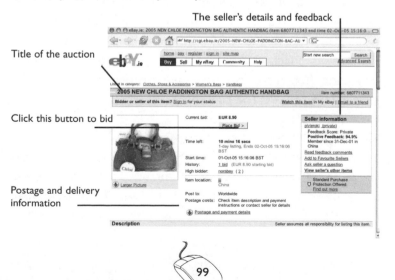

The seller's details and feedback

Title of the auction

Click this button to bid

Postage and delivery information

Once you've found an item you fancy, you place a bid and sit back and wait to find out if you're the winner. Remember that when you place a bid on an online auction, you're entering into a legal contract. If you win the auction, you will have to pay the seller the agreed amount.

Online auctions are often conducted over a matter of days, so you usually won't be able to watch the entire auction. eBay sends you an email when something interesting happens (for example, you win the auction, or you are outbid) so you can keep track of what's going on. You can also access the 'My eBay' section of the site at any time to see the status of each auction you're involved in.

☞ **Remember, online auctions are legally binding.** If you win an auction you have to pay, or face the seller's wrath – and maybe prosecution too!

For many items, you may be buying from people all over the world. It's important that you check where the item is physically located, what it will cost to ship it to Ireland, and whether the seller will ship the item here. Some items (such as foods) can't be shipped long distances easily, or at all. The 'Shipping and Payment details' section of an eBay auction page will show you where the item can be shipped and how much it will cost to ship it. This will also tell you what methods of payment the seller accepts. Also remember to check the currency of the auction. The seller usually chooses a currency convenient to them, so you may be bidding in US\$ or GB£. The currency is clearly shown next to the current bid price.

Once the auction finishes, the seller and the winner both get a confirmation email. It's customary for them to exchange emails to agree on details of shipping, payment, etc. Payment for online auctions is typically done using the PayPal service (www.paypal.com). See Sending Money with PayPal, page 104. PayPal allows you to pay someone without having to send them your credit card number, and also gives you some protection if the goods don't arrive. Remember that the goods will only be dispatched once payment is received.

eBAY

Bidding on eBay

eBay uses a system called 'Proxy bidding'. This means that you tell the site the *maximum* amount you're willing to pay. eBay then automatically bids up to this amount, but only as high as necessary. For example, suppose you're bidding on the world's largest cubic zirconium, with a current high bid of €100. You decide that you're willing to bid up to €150, and enter this amount into the 'Maximum bid' box. Once you confirm the bid, eBay may only need to offer €105 to make you the highest bidder. If someone comes along later and bids €110, eBay raises your bid to €115 and so on, but only up to the maximum of €150 that you specified.

The eBay bidding process is actually a little more complicated than this (the full rules are explained in the 'eBay Explained' section of the site) but the most important thing to remember is, enter the absolute maximum amount you're willing to pay, and don't be tempted to raise it later!

Because a bid on an online auction is legally binding, it's a good idea to use eBay's 'Watch List' feature to keep an eye on an auction while you decide whether you really want to bid. Before you place a bid, check how much time is left in the auction. If it's more than a few minutes, consider adding the item to your Watch List by clicking 'Watch this item'. You can come back to the item at any time by accessing the 'My eBay' section.

☞ **No. 1 tip for eBay bidding:** bid the absolute maximum you're willing to pay; the site will take care of the rest.

Trust on eBay

Any time you do business online, you're trusting someone you haven't met to pay you money or send you goods. It's customary for the seller to be paid before they send the goods. That means that if you win an online auction, you're sending money to a stranger and hoping they send you your widget. Scared? Here's how to avoid getting fleeced.

Using PayPal gives you extra protection when you're paying online. First, the seller never sees your credit card details, so you don't have to worry about fraudulent charges. Second, if you're paying for something you won on eBay, PayPal will refund you up to €500 if the goods never arrive (take a look at the PayPal site for details on which items are covered).

Be especially careful of payment by money transfers since they offer little protection against auction fraud. If a seller *only* accepts payment by money transfer, consider buying elsewhere!

To help you decide which people to trust, eBay uses a system of **Feedback**. Every time someone buys or sells, they can rate the other person as positive or negative. This lets buyers and sellers check how trustworthy the other is based on past transactions. Good buyers will have a high feedback rating, with few negative ratings. You can also check a seller's history to see if they've sold items like this regularly, and see how long they've been a registered member.

☞ **Buying safely on eBay**

- Check the seller's feedback and history; good sellers will have been around for a while and have almost all positive ratings.
- Pay using PayPal, especially if the seller uses the 'Buyer Protection' program.
- Be extra vigilant when buying high-value goods like electronics or computer equipment.

Some sellers use an optional **Buyer Protection** program (look for the logo on their auctions) which gives you even more protection.

Fraud can happen in online auctions; when it does, it's most often associated with high-value items like digital cameras or laptops so be especially careful when buying these items. Beware deals that seem too good to be true – they probably are!

Selling on eBay

Selling your stuff on eBay is simple, too. To get started, just click on the 'Sell' button at the top of the eBay home page. eBay takes you step-by-step through the process of describing your item.

Be careful to set a 'reserve price' if you don't want to sell the item for less than a certain amount. However, eBay will charge you an 'insertion fee' (up to €3) based on this price, regardless of whether the item sells.

If you can, get a digital picture of the item you're selling. eBay will let you upload the picture and will show it on the auction. Including a picture makes people much more confident about doing business with you and will encourage more people to bid. You can choose to have a larger picture, or a box around your listing, for an extra fee.

On the 'Payment and Postage' page, eBay asks you for important information about how a winning bidder can pay. Make sure you select all the payment methods you're willing to accept (usually PayPal – see page 104 for more details on PayPal). If you want to get paid by some other method, for example by meeting the buyer to receive cash, you can select Other/See Item Description and specify the payment method in the payment instructions further down the page or in the item description.

You also need to specify what countries you'll ship to. You might prefer only to deal with buyers in certain parts of the world, but keep in mind that this will limit the pool of potential bidders. You should also specify how you're willing to ship the item, and what cost this will add. You need to be careful to specify sufficient charges for international postage if you're accepting international bidders.

Finally, you can preview your listing to see how it will look. eBay will also calculate the charges for your listing, based on the options you've selected. If you want to change anything, click 'Back' at the bottom of the page. Remember that in addition to the charges shown, you will be charged a 'Final Value Fee' if the item does sell. This is a percentage of the selling price, starting at around five per cent for items that sell for up to €50 and dropping down for more expensive items.

For more information on buying and selling on eBay, pick up a copy of *EBay for Dummies* by M. Collier.

8. SENDING MONEY WITH PAYPAL

As people started to use the internet for buying and selling more often, they needed a way to send money online securely. Credit cards work well when you're dealing with an established merchant, but what if you want to send money to someone you don't know? For example, you might be renting a holiday apartment that you found on www.rentalo.com. Or you might have won an auction for a vintage Elvis vinyl record on www.ebay.ie. Either way, you need to send money to an individual, possibly on the other side of the world, who you've never met, and whose identity you probably can't verify. Sending them you credit card number is a really bad idea. That's where PayPal comes in.

PayPal (now owned by eBay) is a service that lets you send and receive money to or from anyone with an email address. Once you sign up, you register you credit card details with PayPal. If you use PayPal to send someone money, it goes into their PayPal account but they never see your credit card details.

To sign up with PayPal, go to www.paypal.ie and click the 'Sign Up' link to start the process. As a personal user, it's free to sign up with PayPal and there's no charge to send or receive money.

The PayPal home page at www.paypal.ie

Today, PayPal is used by millions of people worldwide to pay for goods and services. Many small businesses use it to get paid quickly, and many individuals and charities use PayPal as a way of collecting small donations on their web sites.

So, what happens when someone sends you money with Pay-Pal? You'll get an email from PayPal telling you that someone has sent you a payment, along with instructions on having that payment added to your PayPal account (you'll have to open a PayPal account if you don't have one). Once the money is in your PayPal account, you can leave it there if you plan to send money to someone else using PayPal, or you can have the money sent to your Irish bank account. To 'withdraw' the money into your bank account, access your PayPal account and go to the 'Withdraw' section. Here you can register your bank account details and request that your PayPal balance be sent to your bank account. It's free to withdraw over €100. For smaller withdrawals there's a €1 fee (check the PayPal web site for the latest fees).

PayPal also gives you some protection against fraud; if you pay for an item that you won on eBay through PayPal, you may be covered for up to €500 if the item doesn't arrive or isn't what you bought. However, there are quite a few exclusions to this policy; see the section on 'PayPal Buyer Protection' in the PayPal web site's 'Help' section. Even if you're not elegible for this scheme,

PayPal will still offer to help you get your money back if you're the victim of fraud, although they don't guarantee that you'll be fully compensated.

Despite being a widely-used service all over the world, and being by far the most common way to pay for online auctions, PayPal does have its detractors, who claim that PayPal can be somewhat arbitrary about some of its policies. These include freezing your accounts if there's any hint of a fraudulent card being used. Some of PayPal's terms and conditions have also been highlighted as allegedly being consumer-unfriendly. For more information on this point of view, you can see www.paypalsucks.com.

Sending money securely at www.paypal.ie

Common sense warning

PayPal can be a convenient way to send money to someone you don't know and in some cases it might give you some protection against fraud. You should always remember that sending money to an individual in another country (or even within Ireland) can be a risky business. You should use some of the same 'common sense' principles that I talk about on page 72 for online shopping: try and find out as much as you can about the seller before sending payment, and try and establish their physical address or contact numbers in case you do have problems. Be especially vigilant if you're sending money outside of Europe and the US.

If you're entering into a large transaction, consider using an escrow service like www.escrow.com. For a small fee, they hold the money until the goods have been received and inspected. (Only use a reputable, *bona fide* escrow service; there have been reports of some fraudsters inventing bogus escrow services to trick people out of money.)

Chapter Four

PROTECTING YOURSELF ONLINE

Being online can be informative, entertaining and really useful. But there are also a few 'gotchas' that can ruin your online experience, lighten your wallet, or worse. Most of these can be avoided with some precaution and a healthy dose of common sense. In this section I'll go through some of the most common concerns that people have when going online and talk about how to keep you, your computer and your family safe online.

1. VIRUSES

WHAT ARE THEY?

Computer viruses are one of the most annoying nuisances of being online. I know people who are so scared of getting a virus on their PC that they're in a perpetual state of terror every time they log on. It's important to protect your computer from viruses, but don't let them stop you getting the most out of the internet.

Some basic facts about viruses:
- They're just small programs written by malicious people (mainly teenage boys) to cause havoc; they didn't 'evolve' on their own and they're generally quite simplistic.
- Different types of malicious programs have different names, including 'trojans' and 'worms'. Most people call them all viruses.
- Some viruses can delete files or otherwise disrupt your computer, but most of them just want to spread to as many other computers as possible. So if you do get a virus, don't panic — your data could be fine.

- The most common way to get a virus is through email. Viruses spread in 'attachments' (files sent along with an email). Viruses can spread in other ways too though.

☞ **Do you have a virus?**

The most common symptoms of having a computer virus are:

- Your computer is suddenly running a lot slower than it used to.
- Your computer suddenly starts to crash a lot more than usual.
- Your internet connection suddenly seems really slow.
- Other things can cause these symptoms too, but if you notice any of these things it's worth checking your computer for viruses.

Viruses often arrive in emails purporting to be from someone you know. Often, the alleged sender of the email wasn't involved at all – the virus has simply found their email address and your email address on an infected computer. When you open the attachment, you infect your computer.

A map of computer virus infections at www.trendmicro.com

Because of how viruses spread, the most important way to protect yourself is not to open suspicious attachments, especially ones that you're not expecting. If you get a suspicious attachment, contact the sender and ask them if it's really from them. Remember – if a stranger handed you a package on the street and asked you to open it, you'd be suspicious. It's the same thing with files you receive by email.

ANTIVIRUS SOFTWARE

Most people choose to install some kind of antivirus software on their computer. New computers increasingly come with antivirus software like Norton Antivirus or McAfee preinstalled.

> ☞ Antivirus software works by running in the background and checking each file you use for signs of known viruses. If it spots something suspicious, it alerts you and tries to remove the virus.

So if you have antivirus software, you're safe, right? Wrong! The most important thing to remember about antivirus software is that it can only protect you from viruses that it knows about. New viruses come out literally every day. To make sure you're protected, you need to ensure that your antivirus software is up to date and knows about the latest threats to your computer. Most software will automatically check for updates when you go online, or you can check manually.

Remember that in addition to buying the software itself, you have to pay a subscription fee to receive the latest updates for your antivirus software. When you buy an antivirus package, or if you buy a new computer that comes with antivirus software, an introductory subscription is usually included. This means that your software will receive updates for a set period of time, usually ninety days or one year. After that, the software will start to complain and ask you to re-subscribe. This usually costs around €10–€20 for a year, and is paid online using a credit card.

Although having to pay this fee every year may seem like an annoyance, **keeping your antivirus up to date is one of the most important things you can do to protect your PC**. If you want to save on subscription fees, use the free AVG software (described below), but don't leave your computer unprotected.

Free antivirus software at free.grisoft.com

The most popular antivirus software is listed below. When you're shopping for antivirus software, be wary of companies trying to sell you 'upgrades' or 'bundles' containing firewall software or other add-ons. If you have a modern computer, these usually aren't worth the extra cost since many of these features come built into Windows. See page 115 for more on firewalls.

AVG   (www.grisoft.com)
As well as the excellent (and low-cost) AVG Professional anti-virus, AGV also provides a good free alternative called AVG Free Edition. You can download it directly from free.grisoft.com and it won't cost you a cent.

McAfee   (uk.mcafee.com)
McAfee's VirusScan product is an excellent alternative and can be downloaded from the McAfee web site. They also have a 'scan my PC' feature if you want to quickly check your computer for viruses.

Symantec   (www.symantec.ie)

Symantec Antivirus has long been the industry standard for virus protection. It can occasionally be problematic to install, so I recommend buying the CD version which gets sent to you in the post rather than the downloadable online edition. It's also widely available in computer shops.

Trend Micro   (www.antivirus.com)

You can buy and download their antivirus software directly from their site. Trend also has a free site that can check your computer for viruses remotely. You don't even need to install any software (but it doesn't work on Macs). This is great if you think you might have picked up a virus and need to check quickly. The address of the site is housecall.trendmicro.com.

SOFTWARE UPDATES

Some viruses infect your computer through bugs in the software running on the computer, or security problems with Windows, the operating system of the computer itself. To make sure you always have the latest version of the operating system, you need to check for updates. Follow these steps to keep your operating system up to date:

If you use Windows, you should regularly run 'Windows Update', which is usually found in your Start menu. Windows Update checks for updates of your Windows software and installs them if necessary.

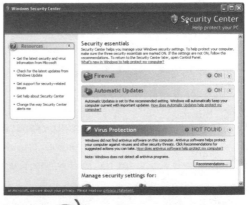

Automatic Updates
in Windows

It's easy to forget to run Windows Update, so you can set it to run automatically. To do this, go to the Start menu, select 'Control Panels' and then 'Security Centre'. Make sure 'Automatic Updates' are turned on.

Configuring software updates on your Mac

If you use an Apple computer, you can use the 'Software Update' program, which is located in the Apple menu. To set your computer to check for updates automatically, select the 'Preferences' option from the 'Software Updates' menu. Here you can set how often the system checks for updates ('Daily' is a good choice). When new updates are available, you'll get a message on the screen.

2. HACKERS AHOY

WHAT ARE THEY?

You can't watch a news report about the internet these days without hearing about the teams of bloodthirsty hackers chomping at the bit, just waiting to break into your computer and steal your precious emails. Like a lot of media coverage of the internet, most hacker stories are incredibly hyped up.

Serious hackers do exist; there are individuals and online groups who break into companies' servers, usually to steal credit card numbers from online store web sites. Some hackers steal trade secrets and try and sell them back to the victims. Others just want to get free goods or services for themselves.

In reality however, most 'hackers' are teenage boys (yes, they are almost all boys) who read a couple of web sites about hacking and decide to try it themselves. These people are often called 'script kiddies' by internet engineers, since they simply download prewritten scripts and try to run them, with little understanding of what the scripts do.

Good and bad hackers

Before it acquired its current sinister connotations, the word 'hacker' was used as a compliment to describe anyone with a lot of in-depth technical knowledge about the internet. Some long-time internet experts still refer to themselves as 'hackers' with pride, although they often clarify that they're good hackers ('white-hat hackers') and not bad hackers ('black-hat hackers').

Unfortunately, 'bad' hackers can still be a threat to your computer. Keep in mind that unless you're particularly famous or important, hackers are rarely interested in your particular computer or files. Even if they were, it's quite difficult for a hacker to find your exact computer on the internet. What hackers do want are computers that they can control remotely. They can then use these computers (known as '**zombies**') to send out spam email messages, or attack a high-profile computer, without it being traced back to them.

So although hackers are unlikely to be interested in copying or deleting your files, they may still attempt to access your computer and turn it into a zombie, to be used for a nefarious purpose in the future. If this happens, you may notice your computer getting extremely slow when you go online. If your computer is being used to send spam emails, your ISP may actually receive complaints and notify you.

To find suitable zombie computers, a hacker waits for a security problem to be discovered in a common piece of software, like Microsoft Windows or Internet Explorer. The hacker then scans thousands of online computers for this vulnerability using automated tools. In some cases, these security problems will allow a hacker to take over a computer.

Stopping hackers is a lot like stopping viruses (see page 108). You need to keep your software up to date and be sure not to open suspicious email attachments. You should also enable a *firewall* on your computer. A **firewall** is a program that screens connections to your computer and rejects any suspicious ones. Firewall software comes built-in with modern versions of Windows XP and MacOS. If you don't have firewall software on your computer, you can buy a program like Norton Internet Security, which contains a virus scanner and a firewall combined.

Enabling your firewall

A firewall can be an important part of your online defences, but you have to make sure it's running first! In Windows, go to the Start menu, select 'Control Panels' and then 'Security Centre' (if you don't have that option, your version of Windows may be too old to have firewall software built in). Make sure that 'Firewall' is on.

If you're using a Mac, go to the Apple menu and choose 'System Preferences' Select the 'Sharing' icon and click the 'Firewall' button. Make sure that 'Firewall On' comes up.

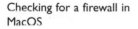

Checking for a firewall in
MacOS

Checking for a firewall in
Windows

Like many online threats, don't let the possibility of hackers take the fun out of going online. If you take the precautions listed in this section, the dangers are pretty low. If you do suspect you've been hacked, don't panic! Disconnect from the internet (hackers can only get you when you're online) and seek help – see page 37 for suggestions on how to get professional help.

☞ The most important things you can do to avoid being vulnerable are:

- Make sure you regularly update your software to protect against security issues. See page 112 for details on how to do this.
- Never open suspicious email attachments. Hackers can use malicious attachments to access your computer, in the same way that viruses spread through email. See page 108 for more details.
- Enable a firewall on your computer.

---

3. SPYWARE

'Spyware' is a type of software that runs in the background and does something (usually annoying) that's calculated to make money for its creator. For example, some spyware will automatically take you to a particular product's web site each time you start your web browser.

Spyware usually gets installed onto your computer by accident, or by your being tricked into installing it; for example, some seemingly legitimate software that you can download from the internet for free actually contains spyware. When you install the program you've downloaded, it surreptitiously installs the spyware, too (some of these programs actually tell you they're installing the spyware – buried in the long licence agreement you have to click 'OK' to).

Although spyware is usually nothing more than an annoyance, it can cause problems by interrupting your normal browsing. To remove spyware from your computer, try using a free tool such as Ad-Aware, available from www.lavasoftusa.com/software/adaware/

Be careful of other programs that claim to remove adware: some of these are actually 'trojan horse' programs that install more adware!

> ☞ Scan your computer for adware every few weeks with a tool such as AdAware.

4. POP-UP WINDOWS

Web sites sometimes open small 'pop-up' web browser windows containing ads. Some (unscrupulous) web sites also try and stop you leaving their site by opening unwanted pop-up windows on your screen. If pop-ups are interfering with your browsing, you can turn them off.

If you've started using Firefox as your browser (see page 129) you can turn off all pop-ups by going to the Preferences menu and choosing 'Web Features', then selecting 'Block Popup Windows'.

If you use Internet Explorer, you can block pop-ups by going to the Tools menu, selecting 'Pop-up Blocker' and making sure the blocker is turned on.

Some sites need pop-ups to work properly. If you have problems just turn the pop-up blocker off. You can also add the site to a special list of sites that are allowed to open pop-ups. In Firefox, this option appears at the top of the screen whenever a pop-up is blocked. In Internet Explorer, go to the Tools menu and select 'Pop-up Blocker' and 'Pop-up Blocker Settings' to configure the blocker.

Turning on the pop-up blocker
in Internet Explorer

117

5. SCAMS AND FRAUD EMAILS

Won the lottery lately? You might think so if you believe some of the emails I get. In addition to winning the lottery several times a day, I also get regular emails from people wanting to transfer large volumes of cash out of their country through my account, as well as several other 'too good to be true' scams.

All of these work in the same way: you're promised a huge payout with absolutely no risk. All you have to do is fill out some forms, or receive and forward some cash, or something similarly innocuous. If you fall for the scam, you'll end up being asked to pay a 'local tax', or 'transfer fee', or some other fictitious charge, in order to receive your huge payout. Since the fee you have to pay is usually a few thousand euro and the payout is usually several million, a surprising number of people fall for this. Needless to say, the payout promptly disappears, along with your money.

These ripoffs are known as 'advance fee fraud' and include variations such as needing to pay a small fee to release something valuable from a warehouse, or bribe a local official to let something through customs. Historically, a large number of these internet scams have originated in Nigeria, leading to the term 'Nigerian Scam' or '419 Scam' being applied to anything of this nature (419 is the section of the Nigerian Criminal Code that outlaws these things). The true origin of this type of confidence trick stretches back way before the internet though, to a scam called the 'Spanish Prisoner Letter' which was carried out via ordinary mail as far back as the sixteenth century.

The basic rule of thumb to avoid being caught by something like this is:

If it sounds too good to be true, it probably is.

No matter what your view of human nature, you should be sceptical of strangers who approach you anywhere, let alone on the internet, offering you millions of euro for doing nothing. Although this may sound obvious, a large number of people (including some from Ireland), have fallen victim to 419 scams. As far back as late 2000, the Garda Bureau of Fraud Investigation reported receiving twenty complaints a month, with one case involving Irish people paying out over £100,000. The scams occasionally have a more sinister element too: some victims have been lured to Nigeria and robbed, or worse.

For more information, see the web site of the 419 Coalition at home.rica.net/alphae/419coal/. They have links to law enforcement agencies and tips on what to do if you do get involved in a 419 scam. If you're the victim of a 419 scam, you can contact the Garda Bureau of Fraud Investigation at 01-666 3777.

6. PHISHING

'Phishing' is a recent type of internet scam that involves trying to trick you into revealing credit card numbers or bank details. Phishing scams are mostly perpetrated by email: you get what looks like a legitimate email from a financial institution asking you to validate your PIN, account number, or other confidential information. These emails are quite sophisticated and usually have 'real' logos from the financial institution. Needless to say, any details you enter will vanish onto the internet and be used by criminals.

Early phishing scams didn't affect many people here since they tended to impersonate big US banks. Recently though, enterprising criminals have been impersonating Irish banks and credit card companies to try and trick us. Phishing emails can also impersonate any online service, like eBay, that might ask for your credit card details.

To protect yourself from phishing scams, follow these guidelines:
• Don't click on links in an email; although they may look legitimate, they may be doctored to take you to a fake site or download a virus. Instead, type the address of your bank's web site (e.g. www.aib.ie) directly into your web browser.
• If you get any suspicious email from a financial institution (or

any other company) asking you to enter any account details or PINs, contact them directly by phone or email to check that it's legitimate.

• Remember that legitimate web sites will never ask you to send PINs or any confidential information by email.

Some web-based email systems will mark some phishing attempts as suspicious. Be particularly careful of emails like this!

> ☞ The Irish Payment Services Organisation runs a web site (www.safecard.ie) to help you protect your bank cards from fraud.

7. YOUR PRIVACY ONLINE

More and more web sites require you to register with them in order to use all the site's features. Although registration is usually free, do you ever wonder what they do with the information you provide? Reputable web sites will publish a 'Privacy Policy' that explains exactly how they use this information. This should be prominently displayed on the page where you register.

Usually, a privacy policy will tell you whether the web site sells or rents its customer list to other companies; this can be important if you don't want to receive ads from other companies.

'A phishing attempt'

In addition to the privacy policy, check what options you have when you register for a web site. There will often be a tick box asking whether you want to receive the web site's newsletter, or ads from that site or other companies.

For more information on protecting your privacy online, visit these web sites:

www.eff.org/Privacy/eff_privacy_top_12.html The Electronic Frontier Foundation's Top 12 tips for safeguarding your privacy online.

www.epic.org The Electronic Privacy Information Centre has lots of in-depth information about privacy issues online; the site can be heavy going though.

8. KIDS AND THE INTERNET

Keeping children safe on the internet is usually the number one issue for parents when they consider going online. Recent media reports about sex offenders using the internet to trade child pornography, or even to meet children, have made parents more aware that children need special protection online.

The internet is like a big city: there are parts of it that are fun, educational, and a fantastic place for kids. And there are other parts that you would never let your kids near. Just like in a real community, most people online are helpful, friendly and honest. But there are also a small minority of creeps, weirdos and criminals.

The key to successful internet use for children is to allow them to access as much of the good stuff as possible, while protecting them from the shadier elements. This section will help give you the tools to do that.

Remember that the internet is just a method of communicating, like the telephone. Criminals do not exist *because* of the internet, but some criminals do use the internet for bad things –

although many more use the phones or the postal service to commit crimes.

One of the most important things you can do to protect your children is to be involved in their online time. Be aware of what they're doing online, just like you'd be aware of what they're watching on TV. A simple but effective way to start doing this is to move your computer into a family room. This helps turn web browsing from something private into a family activity.

In addition, you need to understand what your children are doing when they're online. Since kids who grow up with computers often understand them much better than those of us learning about computers at a later stage, this can be a challenge. But it's vitally important that you know what your kids are up to on the Net. Discuss the sites they're visiting and what they're doing online. If they're using a piece of software that you don't recognise, ask them to explain it to you. If you're not sure, do your own research before allowing them to use it.

Most of what I discuss in the rest of this section is based on the assumption that you keep an eye on what your children are doing online. The younger they are, the more important this is.

* Remember, there are no quick technical fixes to protect your children!

PROTECTING YOUR CHILD FROM CRIMINALS

Broadly speaking, there are two types of things that parents want to avoid online. First, there's the issue that often occupies the public spotlight: the fear that a paedophile may use the internet to contact your children. While this is (thankfully) much less common than media reports often imply, it is a real fear for parents. It's especially of concern when you have younger children who may be more trusting of people they encounter online. Luckily, there are some simple measure that you can take to help prevent any unwanted contact with your kids online.

122

Remember that when your children are surfing the web, they are usually simply reading pages on a web site. This is a relatively low-risk activity. To develop a relationship of trust with your child, a criminal needs a way to *interact* with them. This usually happens through a **chat room** or **message board** (read page 86 for a description of what these are and how they work) or sometimes through email. Because criminals need the interactive elements of chat to operate, you should be especially careful if your children use these types of sites or programs.

It's important to keep in mind that internet criminals who target children generally don't need to be technically sophisticated. It's very difficult for them to find out where you live or your kids' names by technical means. Instead, they build up a relationship with kids over time and simply *ask*. Because of this, the most important rule to set for your children online is:

> Never, ever give out personal information like your last name, address, school or phone number online. If someone pushes you to give this information, or makes you feel uncomfortable in any way, talk to your parents immediately.

Sticking to this simple rule can be extremely effective. However, because of the inherent dangers involved in online chat rooms, some parents ban their use altogether, especially for younger children. The exceptions are chat sites especially designed for kids, where an adult monitors the chat room to ensure appropriate behaviour. For an example, try the monitored chat room at www.kidscom.com.

☞ **Top child safety tips online**
- Keep the computer in a family room.
- Write down simple rules about personal information and post them next to the computer
- Talk to your kids about their internet use and make going online a family activity

For more information on this topic, I recommend visiting the site www.safekids.com. This is a great resource with lots of information on keeping your children safe online. (They also have a sister site, www.safeteens.com, for parents of older children.) Look for their 'Kids Rules For Online Safety', and put a copy next to your computer!

The Irish government's Internet Advisory Board occasionally publishes information guides for parents on their web site, www.iab.ie.

Guidelines for children and parents are available on www.safekids.com

FILTERING OUT ADULT SITES

The second issue that often concerns parents is children accessing adult material, either by accident or on purpose. This is also an issue for older children; never underestimate the ingenuity of a teenage boy trying to access nudie pictures.

Many people ask about technical fixes to this problem: is there software that can filter out adult sites? The simple answer is yes, there is software that will attempt to do this. However, it's important to understand the limits and drawbacks of 'filter' programs before rushing out to buy them.

Filter software generally works like this: you install the software onto your computer having bought it in a shop or down-loaded it from the internet. The software attempts to monitor all access to the internet, and blocks sites it deems 'bad'. The filter software usually has different levels of access, so that young children will be blocked from many sites, while the adults may bypass the filters altogether. Some software also allows you to deny access to different categories of sites based on the topic (gambling, sex, games, etc.).

To decide which sites are 'bad', filtering software relies on two types of tests. At the most basic level, the software company will have a room full of people paid to find and categorise adult sites (no, I don't know where you apply for that job). The software installed on your computer periodically downloads a list of banned sites from a central server and updates itself.

Some software will also try and make more sophisticated guesses about a web site based on its content. When you access a site, the software will scan it for words like 'sex', and prevent access if it thinks the page is naughty.

There are a few problems with these approaches. The first is that at some level, you're relying on someone else to make judgements about the sites your kids will be allowed to visit. If their view of what's appropriate is not the same as yours, you might not be happy with the results.

Because of this, many filtering programs err on the side of

A site blocked using CyberPatrol

caution and ban a lot of sites that you might not expect. This can be made worse when sites are rejected because of words that they contain. There are many stories of sites dealing with sexual health; birth control; and especially breast cancer, falling afoul of the filters. This can be a problem with teenage children, who may look to the internet for information on topics they may not want to discuss at home.

Controversially, some filtering software also filters sites of a political nature … and sometimes only sites supporting one side of an issue.

Filtering software can also lull parents into a false sense of security. New web sites spring up all the time and it can take a while for the software to become aware of the latest ones. But having installed filtering software, some parents then feel that they don't need to keep an eye on children's internet usage, not realising that no filtering software will block one hundred per cent of bad sites. Also, it's important to remember that no software is impenetrable, and a determined, computer-savvy teenager can find ways to disable or bypass many obstacles standing between them and a web site. Lastly, filtering software may undermine the element of trust regarding internet usage, making children less likely to come to you if they do come across a site that they're not comfortable with.

Having said all that, filtering software can play a role in protecting your kids, especially in the case of younger children. Younger kids are more likely to stumble upon an adult site by accident, since they may follow a link or advertisement without realising what they're about to access. Also, younger children are less likely to be accessing the kind of sites that filtering software may block by accident.

If you think that filtering software is appropriate as part of your strategy for protecting your children, here are the two most popular filter programs. Both currently provide free trials, and you can download the software directly from their web sites. Of the two, I prefer Net Nanny for home use:

126

www.cyberpatrol.com

www.netnanny.com

CHILD PORNOGRAPHY

Many people are worried about accidentally viewing or down-loading child pornography on the internet. The good news is that coming across this sort of material by accident is extremely un-likely. Possession of child pornography, online and offline, is a crime that is taken extremely seriously by police forces in most of the western world, including the gardaí (although unfortunately not in some parts of Asia and Eastern Europe). The gardaí have raided many homes and offices in connection with possession of this kind of material, and regularly arrest and prosecute offend-ers. This means that groups who have illicit material like this usu-ally operate in great secrecy, vetting potential members before allowing access. They rarely if ever advertise or draw attention to themselves for fear of prosecution.

I'm regularly asked if a virus or hacker can put illegal material on your computer. Although this could technically be possible, I've never come across it. Again, remember that people trafficking in illegal material are usually paranoid about secrecy and are

Report child pornography at www.hotline.ie

more likely to charge for access to their material than to force it on you for nothing.

There is, however, a lot of adult material on the internet, and it's not hard to click on an adult site by mistake. If this happens, don't panic! Just close your browser window or click 'Back'. If you do find material that you think may be illegal, you can report it to the Hotline, run by the Internet Service Providers Association of Ireland. It is available at www.hotline.ie. The Hotline staff will investigate and pass on the information to the authorities in Ireland or the country where the site is hosted. Bear in mind that the Hotline only deals with *illegal* materials, such as child pornography, rather than material which is adult in nature but not illegal.

('Legitimate' adult sites hosted in the US are required to adhere to a law known as 18 U.S.C. 2257, and place a '2257 compliance notice' on the site, stating that all models are over 18, and listing the location where supporting records are kept, and by whom. Recent changes in US law make these requirements even more stringent.)

Still worried?
Don't let the dangers outlined in this section of the book keep you from going online. It's important that you understand the potential pitfalls of venturing into the online world but remember that by taking a few basic precautions you can have a safe, educational and, most importantly, fun time on the Net. Jump on in and enjoy it.

APPENDIX: INSTALLING FIREFOX

Firefox is a free web browser that many people choose to install instead of Internet Explorer. It provides additional security and is considered less vulnerable to viruses, phishing and spyware. You can happily have both Firefox and Internet Explorer installed and choose which you want to launch each time you browse the web. Installing Firefox is easy:

1. Using Internet Explorer, go to www.getfirefox.com.
2. Click on the 'Download' link.
3. You will be asked where to save the downloaded file; save it somewhere easy to find on your hard disk, like your desktop.
4. Wait for the file to download fully (this will take between thirty seconds and half an hour, depending on the speed of your connection).
5. Find the downloaded file and double-click on it.
6. The installer will guide you through the installation steps.
7. You should now have a stylish 'Firefox' icon on your desktop.
8. Double-click to launch Firefox.
9. Surf the web!

The first time you launch Firefox, it will ask you if you want it to be your default web browser; it doesn't really matter what you choose here; you can always decide to launch either Firefox or Internet Explorer by double-clicking its icon on your desktop.

> ☞ **Firefox** is produced by volunteer programmers whose work is co-ordinated by the non-profit Mozilla Foundation. Their efforts are motivated by a desire to create a better, faster and safer web browser. This is one example of the increasingly common phenomenon of free or 'Open Source' software. Rather than being produced by a corporation, many pieces of software are now written by volunteers and released for free on the internet. For more information about the Open Source movement, see www.opensource.org

4. PROTECTION

Chapter Five

WEB DIRECTORY
GREAT SITES TO GET
YOU STARTED

ABOUT THIS DIRECTORY

The web is a huge, amorphous and everchanging beast. The sites here are ones I've found over the years. Some of them I like, some I use every day and some are just plain weird. For each topic below, there are probably a dozen more equally good sites that aren't listed. If you find one you particularly like, let me know (you can contact me through my web site, www.internetguide.ie). The problem with putting a list of web sites in a book is that sites occasionally close down, change address or go out of business. To keep up to date with the latest sites, keep an eye on my web site. I post updates, corrections and new sites there all the time.

Banking

All the major Irish banks have online functionality that allows you to view your balance and pay bills online. This can be a huge time-saver! Many banks allow you to apply for loans, mortgages and credit cards online and some offer you discounts for going through their web sites. (See page 70 on security if you're worried about whether this is safe.)

www.aib.ie
AIB's web site, including online banking.

www.365online.com
Bank of Ireland's online banking portal.

www.anytime.ulsterbank.com
Bank online with Ulster Bank.

www.open24.ie
Permanent TSB's online banking site.

www.mbna.ie
Apply for a credit card and access your MBNA credit card account online.

Books

www.amazon.co.uk
Amazon is arguably the web site that made online shopping famous – and easy. Amazon is known for its online bookstore (still the most comprehensive bookstore you'll see anywhere) but it also carries a range of other things, from CDs to garden furniture. The UK web site will ship most small items to Ireland for reasonable rates, although pricing is in sterling. This is probably the safest place on the Net to shop.

Find Irish books at
www.kennysirishbookshop.ie

www.kennysirishbookshop.ie
Ireland's leading online bookshop. Kenny's used to be a real bookshop too, but it is now exclusively online. They sell popular Irish books as well as hard-to-find Irish-interest items.

www.abebooks.com

This site brings buyers and sellers of books together. This is great for finding out of print or rare books, too. Bear in mind that you're buying directly from individual sellers (many of them specialist book dealers) so shipping rates to Ireland will vary. Try its Book Sleuth feature – it helps you find a book even if you can't remember its name or author. (For schoolbooks, see the Education listings below.)

Clothes and Fashion

www.asos.com

Buy the clothes your favourite celebrities wear from the As Seen On Screen web site. This site has replicas of clothes seen on people like David Beckham, Kate Moss and Cat Deeley but at high-street prices. Shipping to Ireland is quick and cheap.

www.shoes.com

Lots of shoe labels are going online. This site has a huge range of shoes from popular brands like Merrell, Ugg and Timberland. They ship to Ireland for a reasonable price and you'll find many ranges and models not available in Ireland. (I just got a cool pair of blue Sketchers from this site.)

www.style.com

The online home of *Vogue* magazine ... tons of content not in the magazine, including new season previews.

www.cafepress.com

Cafe Press allows anyone to create their own line of t-shirts, shorts, tops and mugs. They carry items from hundreds of thousands of amateur designers, bands, etc.

Cooking, Food and Drink

www.epicurious.com

Epicurious is fun because people can add comments and suggestions about the recipe. Very democratic. They also have some of my favourite pizza recipes!

www.RecipeZaar.com

Another good recipe and cooking site ... but it wouldn't be the web without some strange stuff, so they also have some 'alternative' recipes, like Fresh Figs and Cream pancakes. Mmmmm ... figs.

www.webtender.com

The ultimate guide to cocktail recipes on the web. As well as details on how to make every conceivable drink, you can also tell it what ingredients you have, and it tells you what you can make! (That's at www.webtender.com/cgi-bin/imbselect). I use this site all the time!

Find out what you can mix up at www.webtender.com

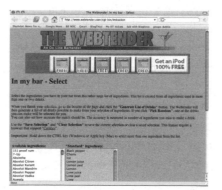

Dating and Chat

www.maybefriends.com
Irish dating site with 15,000 registered members. They have live chat and organise monthly real-life meetings for people to meet up.

www.hotornot.com
Find out how other people see you: you upload a picture and other people can rate you from 1–10. They also have a 'Meet Me' service so you can email people you like the look of. They make tens of thousands of matches every twenty-four hours. The Meet Me service is at meetme.hotornot.com.

www.cupid.ie

A site for the teenager in all of us: Do you have a crush on some-one and wonder if they feel the same? This site lets you find out anonymously.

www.speeddatingireland.com

For people who are too busy to go on proper dates: speed net-working has hit Ireland. Meetings around Ireland, €20 for two hours, during which you meet twenty-five people (four minutes each).

www.friendster.com

This is the biggest of the 'social networking' web sites. Great for meeting people through mutual friends, for work, romance or anything else. When you join, you invite your friends to join, they invite their friends, etc. You create a profile of your interests and activities, and you can see who knows who and get introductions to the people you want to meet. Extremely popular in the US.

chat.yahoo.com

Live chatting online with people all over the world. Dozens of topics, thousands of people. (See chapter three for more infor-mation on online chat.)

DIY

www.woodiesdiy.com

If you need tools or DIY materials, you can get at practically the full range of Woodie's stock online. Cheap delivery across Ireland.

www.diynot.com

Really good step-by-step instructions for common household DIY tasks, like 'How do I wire an electrical socket'. There are also forums where you can ask questions from more knowledgeable DIY-ers.

Education

www.skoool.ie

Despite the funky spelling, this is a good site with study guides, downloadable materials and good course overviews.

www.nightcourses.com

Interested in a night course? This web site has a database of 25,000 night courses all over Ireland, from car maintenance to learning Japanese (yes, there are courses on using the internet, too!).

www.ratemyteachers.ie

Controversial site that allows students to give ratings and feedback to their own teachers. This is great fun if you're trying to pick which courses to do or which grind schools to go to. Since the site is anonymous, there's no guarantee that the ratings aren't influenced by disgruntled students, but a 'moderator' for each school edits and removes unhelpful comments and suspect ratings.

www.schoolbookexchange.ie

Tried of buying new books every year? This site lets you buy and sell used books.

Shop for cheaper schoolbooks at www.schoolbooks.ie

www.schoolbooks.ie

Buy your books new online; good range of books across all subjects, both primary and secondary.

www.buy4now.ie/arnotts

Arnotts' online store sells basic uniform trousers, shirts and jumpers online (select uniforms from the category menu).

Flowers

www.sheilasflowers.com

This is my favourite online florist: they have a good selection of flowers and bouquets, they deliver promptly (even the same day) and they're reliable.

Flowers online at www.madflowers.com

www.madflowers.com

Madflowers has an unusually creative approach to arrangements and offers delivery throughout Ireland and abroad.

Friends and Family

www.myfamily.com

This site is pretty cool … it allows you to set up a web site to keep track of all your family worldwide over the internet, including a calendar of birthdays and shared photo albums.

www.cyndislist.com

Free site with information and tutorials on researching your ancestry and family online. It has a specific section on Ireland. Great place to start learning about genealogy research.

www.friendsreunited.co.uk
Find long-lost friends and schoolmates.

www.ellisisland.org
An example of the free genealogy data that's available on the
internet: view and search records of all the emigrants to the US
who passed through Ellis Island. The full ship manifests are available online to registered users (registration is free).

www.tribalpages.com
Construct a full family tree online, complete with photos, and
share it with your family and friends. The basic service is free.

Gadgets and Networking Equipment

www.engadget.com
Engaget is my favourite site for news and reviews of gadgets of all
sorts, from new mobile phones to handmade wooden computer
keyboards.

www.expansys.ie
Expansys is a UK-based online computer superstore that stocks
the latest mobile phones as well as Wi-Fi networking equipment,
modems and more. They ship to Ireland quickly, cheaply and reli-
ably.

Gambling

Betting online has become a huge industry; whether you're a serious gambler or you just like to make novelty bets, you can do it
all online (think you know who's going to be the next Taoiseach?
Here's your chance to clean up). It's especially handy if you've
never made a bet before … betting online is straightforward and
you don't have to visit a bookie.

www.paddypower.com
Paddy Power is a simple place to start and caters to absolute

beginners as well as more seasoned punters. You can bet on most sports and they also have a good 'Novelties' section where you can bet on things like when men will land on Mars.

Bet on the Rose of Tralee at www.paddypower.com

www.betfair.com
If you fancy yourself as a bookie, this site lets you lay your own odds on all major sporting events, and take bets from people across the internet. Not for the novice.

www.888.com
On of the web's largest online casinos. You can play a range of casino games as well as playing poker against real people online. To play some games you need to download their casino software.

www.gamblersanonymous.org
If you think you have a gambling problem, visit the Gamblers Anonymous web site for help.

Gardening
www.bbc.co.uk/gardening
As well as lots of info, tips and hints, this has a 'Design your virtual garden' tool (in the 'Design' section) with a full 3-D view ... drop

in plants, walls, ponds, etc. and see how your garden would look ... a great tool! (This requires some extra software called Shockwave to be installed on your computer; you can download it from the same site.)

www.rbgkew.org.uk
The Royal Botanic Gardens at Kew have all their information and pictures of their specimens online. You can also buy seeds, cuttings, etc. online.

www.carryongardening.org.uk
A gardening site for people with disabilities and the elderly. Full of advice and tips on how to keep gardening even if you have limited mobility.

www.homeandgardenmakeover.com
Advice on DIY and gardening, plus a weekly email newsletter.

Getting Around
www.dublincity.ie
The notoriously hard to navigate Dublin City Council web site has great info on the traffic situation in Dublin (click 'Getting around'). They have live images from the traffic cameras around the city; information about the city-centre car parks; parking zone information; and notices of any traffic disruptions.

www.dto-journeyplanner.ie
This site draws maps to help you walk or cycle around Dublin, including a handy calorie counter. It also has links to bus and rail timetables.

www.irishrail.ie
Full national rail timetables online, as well as online ticket sales and latest news about disruptions and extra services.

www.luas.ie

Timetable and fare information for the Luas, as well as news and route maps.

Going Out

www.entertainment.ie

A great site for cinema, theatre and music listings. This is always my first stop if I'm heading for the cinema, since they have complete lists as well as reviews.

www.ticketmaster.ie

Love them or hate them, Ticketmaster is the agent for most gigs around Ireland. Their web site is really good, with sections for music, sports and family events. You can buy tickets online (complete with annoying service charge) and have them posted to you or collect them at the venue. This site is a great option for buying popular tickets as soon as they go on sale without having to queue all night! Tickets are completely nonrefundable, so book carefully. eBay is also a great source for tickets for sold-out events ... check out the section on using eBay in chapter three.

Browse restaurant menus at www.diningtreats.com

www.diningtreats.com

Nice well-structured web site with details and menus for a selection of restaurants. Good suggestion section as well as money-off coupons. Only Dublin for the moment, though.

140

www.dublinpubscene.com
Reader reviews of many Dublin pubs, both well-known and off the beaten track.

www.adlib.ie
A good listing of restaurants around the country, rated by cost. Some have their menus online, too. They don't have full reviews of each one unfortunately.

Government Services
The Irish government prides itself on being ahead of many countries in terms of providing 'e-government services' (in other words, having good web sites). In the case of many government departments, this reputation is well-deserved. Here are some of the most useful web sites from local and national government bodies.

www.motortax.ie
Forget queuing for hours or dealing with cryptic forms, you can now renew your car tax online using the PIN sent to you with your renewal notice. You can pay securely using a credit card or Laser card.

www.oasis.gov.ie
Oasis is a big but well-organised web site that aims to pull together information on all sorts of government services on one web site. It does a great job of making a huge amount of information easy to access and simple to understand, from what to do when you have a child to getting a dog licence.

www.revenue.ie
This web site isn't going to make you like paying tax, but it will make it easier. The Revenue is trying to encourage more people to use its online tax service, ROS (for 'Revenue Online Service'), to file common tax returns and pay money owed. You can also

download some useful leaflets and handbooks on common tax issues, such as starting work for the first time or setting up a small business.

Health
There are specialist sites for just about every condition out there; for a good overview site, go to www.drkoop.com (see below) or use Google to find a specialist site.

www.drkoop.com.
This site is run by the former US surgeon general and provides a wide range of information, treatment details and prevention tips for hundreds of common conditions. Since it's US-centric some of the medications or treatments aren't available here, but it's a great place to start.

www.healthhub.ie.
For an Irish perspective, this site provides basic information on health matters in Ireland, including a news section, regular news-letter by email and help finding local services (GPs, blood dona-tion centres, etc.).

www.quackwatch.org
This is one of several sites providing information on health scams, quacks and bogus treatments, allowing you to check up on some-thing before buying a 'miracle cure'.

www.embarrassingproblems.com.
The internet is full of off-beat sites like this one; it answers the questions you're too embarrassed to ask your doctor.

All the major Irish health insurers have their own web sites, pro-viding information for their customers and also some general health information:

www.vhi.ie
www.bupa.ie
www.vivashealth.ie

Job Hunting

In the past few years, the recruitment industry has taken to the internet in a huge way. Most good recruitment firms have web sites where vacancies are updated constantly, and many allow you to upload your CV for employers to search, too. The best of them have free sections to help you build your CV and find the perfect job.

www.monster.ie
Probably the world's largest recuitment site, with online search facilities and over a million jobs worldwide. Pretty good for Ireland, too.

www.recruitireland.com
Sometimes it's good to have a local focus; several Irish recruitment agencies have really good sites, including this one.

www.irishjobs.ie
Another good Irish recruitment site.

www.nixers.ie
As the name implies, this site specialises in casual jobs. They have a lot of service industry listings, as well as jobs in Irish bars abroad.

www.linkedin.com
Job hunting based on 'social networking' – meet friends of friends online to get personal introductions to job vacancies. This is the sort of thing that would never be possible without the internet.

Money-saving Sites

www.irishfuelprices.com

Shows you where to get the best deals on petrol, diesel and home heating oil; it's updated constantly by ordinary shoppers so it's up to date all the time.

frugalliving.about.com

Gives tips on saving money for serious savers, including making your own dog food (tasty!), re-using things around the house, etc.

www.pigsback.com

An Irish site that gives you money-off coupons you can print and use in your local Tesco, Superquinn, etc. The cool thing is that they tailor them to your past purchases (I get coupons for money off Goodfellas pizzas, for example). It's free to register. Can't beat something for nothing!

Music, Movies and Games

The internet is a great place to shop for CDs and DVDs. Besides the sites listed here, remember to check eBay (www.ebay.com) for hard to find or out-of-print items. (For details on downloading music online, see chapter three.)

When buying movies or games, make sure to check the regional encoding and format of the discs; many DVDs will only play in certain parts of the world. Irish DVD players and games consoles use 'Region 2' and 'PAL' encoding, so make sure the discs you're buying support both of these (the US uses 'Region 1' and 'NTSC').

www.cdwow.ie

CD Wow is a great discount superstore for CDs, DVDs and games. They ship from Hong Kong at big discounts compared to high-street stores (often half price) but shipping can take a week or more and the selection is usually limited to popular titles. Free shipping!

www.amazon.co.uk
As well as its pioneering online bookstore, Amazon has a great selection of CDs, DVDs and games. Remember, it's usually cheaper to ship a few things together.

www.sendit.com
Previously known as Blacknight, this longtime UK-based online shop has a great selection of DVDs, with an especially good catalogue of TV series.

launch.yahoo.com
The best place to keep track of your favourite bands, including tour information, free clip downloads and album release news.

News and Weather
Most news organisations put their material up on the web, sometimes before they publish it elsewhere. Some sites charge a subscription fee for access, but many are free.

news.google.com
Google's news site aggregates stories from sites all over the world to show you the most important global news. You can customise the page to show only the sections you're interested in, or even add specific searches ('Irish sports' for example).

Get the forecast at
www.weather.com

www.rte.ie/news
Good breaking news headlines from the RTÉ newsroom (free).
You can also listen to the RTÉ news online.

www.ireland.com
The Irish Times puts almost the whole paper online, plus additional
web-only sections and special features. They charge a subscription fee for full access though (this makes a great present for
relatives living abroad who want to keep up with news at home!).

news.yahoo.com
If you register with Yahoo (free), you can customise your news
page to show only topics that you're interested in, in whatever
order you like.

www.feedreader.com
FeedReader is a piece of Windows software that reads RSS feeds
(basically, news feeds) from news sources worldwide and shows
them on your desktop.

www.weather.com
Need a forecast? Get global weather information, forecasts, ave-
rages and lots of pretty pictures and graphs.

Personal Finance
www.askaboutmoney.com
An Irish discussion board where you can ask anything about personal finance (Where has the cheapest mortgage? What should I
do about my PRSA?) and get lots of answers for free. Great 'best
buys' section for choosing a mortgage or credit card.

www.jeacle.ie/mortgage
Handy tool to graphically calculate how much of your mortgage
goes on interest, how much you save by repaying it early, etc.
Draws pretty pictures!

www.mabs.ie
Independent advice on budgeting and dealing with debts. The service is funded by the Dept of Community and Social Affairs; they also have a nice loan calculator and online budget calculator.

www.fool.com
A great introductory site on all aspects of money and investing. Somewhat US-centric but explains things like bonds, funds and interest rates really clearly.

www.esatclear.ie/~grabe/TaxCalc/TaxCalc.html
Irish tax calculator; works out all the details of your PAYE, PRSI, etc. so you can check your payslips and figure out what a tax break would mean to you.

www.vicefund.com
Recently all sorts of 'ethical investments' have sprung up, where the companies are carefully vetted. This is the opposite: they invest in gambling, alcohol and tobacco companies – and make twenty-five per cent a year doing it!

philip.greenspun.com/WealthClock.Intl
Compare your personal finances to those of Bill Gates, the world's richest man, on the Bill Gates Wealth Clock. Updated 24 hours a day!

Pets
www.pethealthcare.co.uk
This site provides information on the whole range of domestic pets with a good focus on how to choose the first pet for a child. They also have a 'buyer's guide' for each species (hamsters, rabbits, mice, as well as dogs and cats) telling you what to look for when you're buying one.

animal.discovery.com

The Discovery Channel has a huge amount of information on all sorts of animals, including a great dog breed selector (look for the 'Pet Guides and Tools' section). It's a cool way to choose a dog: they ask you ten questions about size, exercise and other doggie issues and then recommend the best breeds for you.

www.bowwowsbest.com

The ultimate in over-the-top accessories for your dog; jewellery, leopard-print beds, designed collars, etc. Crazy expensive, but guaranteed to make your dog look stylish (email them for shipping rates to Ireland).

petsonthego.com

Do you miss your pet when you travel? This site is dedicated to helping you take Fido with you when you go on holidays. They have tips and hints for travelling with a pet as well as a database of 30,000 pet-friendly places to stay.

www.ilovedmypet.com

Only on the internet … This site allows you to create an online memorial to a pet who has died, including pictures, video and stories that you can share with friends. The basic service is free.

Photos

Photos have all gone digital these days (just try buying a non-digital camera if you don't believe me!). These sites will help you do something useful with all those digital pics.

www.flickr.com

Create online photo albums and share them with your friends. Several people can contribute to albums of events (e.g. everyone who was at a wedding can add their own pics to the album).

www.photobox.ie

For getting prints, fridge magnets and t-shirts too!

Property
www.myhome.ie
This site is run by some of Ireland's biggest estate agents and is a great place to start if you're looking for property for sale. They have great mapping features so you can see all the houses available in each neighbourhood. They even have satellite pictures of many properties.

www.daft.ie
DAFT started out specialising in rentals and is still hands down the best site to use to find a place to rent in Ireland. You can deal directly with landlords but agents all list their properties here too. I've found my past three apartments on this site. More recently, they've started listing properties for sale, allowing you to cut out estate agents and deal directly with buyers and sellers.

www.missilebases.com
One of the more 'specialised' selling sites on the web. Sells refurbished US underground missile bases. 45,000 sq feet under Colorado, anyone?

Reference
www.wikipedia.org
A free, community-based encyclopaedia with over 500,000 entries. Anyone can update an article or add a new one.

www.reference.com
This site has an encyclopaedia, atlas, dictionary and more all in one.

maps.google.co.uk
See maps and satellite images of the UK and Ireland.

Sports

Just about every sport you can think of has dozens of web sites dedicated to it, both official sites and fan-run ones. Here's a few to get you started.

www.rugby.ie
The home of all things rugby, from the Heineken Cup to the Six Nations. Full coverage and results.

www.gaa.ie
Slightly disappointing official GAA web site with some news and fixture lists.

www.clubgaa.ie
Provides links to all the local clubs, as well as news and an online discussion forum for each region.

www.worldcup.com
Official football World Cup web site with fixtures, results, news and tickets.

www.wimbledon.org
A great example of what a good sports site can be like; not only can you get full background information on the players and buy tickets online, you can also see a shot-by-shot live scoreboard and shot tracker. Pour yourself a glass of Pimms and you might as well be there!

www.sailingireland.com
The portal for sailing holidays in Ireland. Details of charters, sailing schools, moorings and marinas. Lots of good info about where to go for a sailing break. Darrrr.

www.oceanready.com
A great site that matches boats and crew for races and deliveries. Whether you're an experienced sailor or an absolute novice,

there's a boat out there that needs your help. You can get places on weekend jaunts or even major races.

Weddings

Because weddings are such a huge business, the internet has become a great source of information. Most wedding suppliers (dress designers, venues, travel agents, etc.) have their own web sites, which you can find on Google. There are also a large number of really bad sites which are just trying to cash in on the act (one I visited recently prominently advertises its divorce service!) and many are simply pages and pages of ads, with no useful info at all. The sites below have good, useful content and are genuinely useful (according to my recently-married friends!).

www.weddingsonline.ie
Irish site with good, informative articles and online discussion boards where you can ask questions of other brides-to-be.

www.thebestmansspeech.com
Get suggestions based on the groom's character traits. Funny one-liners, anecdotes, etc.

www.confetti.co.uk
UK/Ireland wedding site with a good directory of services, useful series of articles, and a section just for men.

www.thehitchingpost.co.uk
Cool service that lets you build a mini-site to organise your wedding; UK-centric but that doesn't affect most of the site.

www.weddinglocation.com
If you're planning a wedding abroad, check out this global directory of wedding venues.

www.irishweddinginsurance.ie
If you're a pessimist, you can even buy wedding insurance online.

FURTHER READING

Want more? At this stage, you've mastered using the web for lots of things. And the best place to learn about the internet is … online. Search on Google for the topics that interest you, read some of the tech news sites like Wired (www.wired.com) and of course check out my site at www.internetguide.ie for updates and more cool sites. You can also use my web site to send me your feedback.

But if you want more books about the Net, here are a few good ones (they're all available in most bookstores or online from www.amazon.co.uk):

The Rough Guide Website Directory (Rough Guides) is a nice directory of sites organised by topic. The sites are good, but bear in mind that it's somewhat UK-focused so not all of them are relevant to Ireland (online stores might not ship here, for example).

The Complete Idiot's Guide to Windows XP by Paul McFedries is a good book for brushing up on basic Windows skills, like navigating through menus, organising files and dragging-and-dropping.

Mac OS X Tiger for Dummies by Bob Levitus is perfect for learning how to use your Apple Mac. It covers all the basic skills like using the Finder, moving your files around, and keeping your computer running smoothly.

Windows XP All-in-One Desk Reference for Dummies by Woody Leonhard is the right book for you if you want to learn more about advanced topics, including lots of information about using your Windows computer for advanced internet tasks.

eBay for Dummies by Marsha Collier *et al.* If you're serious about buying or selling on eBay, this book goes into depth on a range of eBay topics from setting up an account to avoiding fraud and making money selling your products on eBay.

Creating Web Pages (Sams Teach Yourself Series) by Preston Gralla and Matt Brown. A great primer if you want to develop your own web site. This book takes you through all the basics including writing HTML, creating professional-looking sites, and uploading the pages to your web server.

GLOSSARY OF TERMS

Access Point
A small device that creates a wireless hotspot within your home or office. It's similar in size to a modem and broadcasts a **Wi-Fi** signal.

ADSL
See **DSL**.

Antivirus software
A program that scans your computer and removes viruses. See also **Virus**.

Blog
A web log, or 'blog', is an online diary where you post your thoughts on anything or everything. The most successful blogs concentrate on a particular topic and have several posts a day.

Broadband
Any fast, always-on internet connection. Although the words 'DSL' and 'broadband' are often confused, DSL is just one type of broadband. See also **DSL**.

Chat room
A service that allows you to 'chat' online with others by typing your messages. Anything you type is seen by others in the chat room as soon as you hit Return.

Dial-up connection
A way of connecting to the internet using an ordinary phone line and a modem. See also **modem**.

Download
The process of getting information or files 'down' from the internet to your computer. See also **upload**.

DSL
Digital Subscriber Line. A fast internet connection that uses your existing phone line. DSL uses different frequencies from normal phone calls, so it doesn't interfere with your telephone. DSL is one type of *broad-*

band. Different types of DSL exist. The most common in Ireland is Asymmetric DSL (ADSL).

Firefox
A free, *Open Source* web browser that you can download. It's generally considered more powerful and secure than Internet Explorer, which comes with most computers.

Fixed wireless
A range of broadband technologies that can connect your home or office to the internet without using your phone line or other wires. Fixed wireless connections usually use a small antenna on the roof of your building.

Google
One of the most popular *search engines* on the internet, located at www.google.ie. Google can help you find lots of useful stuff on the Net.

Hard disk
The main storage space on your computer. The hard disk holds programs, the **operating system**, and the files you save. It is also known as a 'hard drive'.

Hardware
All the physical parts of your computer. Anything you can kick is hardware. Anything you can't is software.

Hotspot
An area where **Wi-Fi** internet access is available. This can be in a public place like a hotel or coffee shop, or in your home or office.

http://
The prefix that goes in front of a web address (a **URL**). It stands for Hyper Text Transfer Protocol and identifies an address as a web address rather than anything else. These days, people usually omit the http:// at the beginning of a URL. Your browser will automatically add it, anyway.

Linux
A free open source operating system commonly found on servers. See also **Open source software**.

Message board

A web site where you can 'post' messages to be read by others, usually related to a specific topic.

Modem

A small device that connects your computer to your phone line for dial-up connections. A 'DSL modem' is used to connect to your phone line for DSL connections. Similarly, a 'cable modem' connects to your cable TV service if you have cable broadband.

Open Source Software

The inner workings of most software is a closely-guarded trade secret to prevent other people copying it. Some software (like Firefox) is re-leased on the internet and anyone can examine its 'source code'. Other programmers can then modify the program and improve it. This is known as Open Source Software. See also **Firefox**.

Operating System

The basic software that runs on a computer and takes care of things like organising files, letting you run programs, etc. The most common operating systems are Windows and MacOS.

Peer-to-peer

A type of networking allowing computers to talk directly to each other without a central server (also known as 'P2P'). Peer-to-peer applications are usually used to share files. They became famous for allowing people to illegally share music and movie files, but are now used for legitimate purposes, too.

Phishing

The process of trying to get sensitive information (credit card numbers, passwords, etc.) by sending you fake emails purporting to be from your bank or a legitimate web site.

Processor

The 'brain' of your computer. It actually does the hard work and data-crunching.

RAM

The temporary memory used by programs and documents that are currently in use. RAM is measured in megabytes (MB) or gigabytes (GB). I GB = 1024 MB.

Search engine
A site that lets you search the web for specific words or phrases. See also **Google**.

Secure site
See **SSL**.

Server
A computer on the internet that provides access to web pages or other files. If you have a web site of your own, it is stored here so that other people can see it.

Snail-mail
What email users call the paper postal service, due to its comparatively slow speed.

Software
The programs that run on your computer. See also **Hardware.**

Spam
Unwanted ads sent you by email. Also known as 'unsolicited commercial email' or UCE.

Spyware
A program that hides on your computer and does something to make money for its author. This can include gathering information on you and sending it back to the author; popping up ads; or forcing your web browser to open certain web sites.

SSL
'Secure socket layer'; a technology that encrypts the traffic between your web browser and the web site you're viewing. This can help protect sensitive information such as your credit card number when you shop online. Sites that use SSL are sometimes called 'secure sites'.

Trojan Horse
See **Virus**.

Upload
The processing of sending data or files 'up' to another computer on the internet. See also **download**.

URL
The address of a web page. Looks like www.internetguide.ie. URL stands for 'Universal Resource Locator'.

Virus
A malicious program that runs on your computer and spreads to other computers. The term virus is generally used to refer to any nasty programs, including worms (which just spread but don't do any damage) and trojan horses (which come disguised as something useful).

Web log
See **Blog**.

Wi-Fi
A technology that allows your computer to connect to the internet without wires. Wi-Fi is commonly found in public **hotspots** or can be used to access your broadband connection around your house or office. Also known as 'wireless LAN' or 'WLAN'.

WiMax
An emerging standard for **Fixed wireless** internet access. It's used by ISPs to connect your house to their network wirelessly.

WLAN
See **Wi-Fi**.

Worm
See **Virus**.

INDEX